9급 공무원 영어 시험대비

박문각 공무원
기 본 서

내 인생 마지막 기본 영어구문

영어 문장을 정확하게 읽는 힘!

폭넓은 어휘 활용법 학습

문장별 문법 KILLER 포인트로 반복 효과

빈출 문장의 패턴화로 영어 자신감 향상

김태은 편저

김태은 영어
마지막 기본 영어구문

동영상 강의 www.pmg.co.kr

박문각

PREFACE

이 책의 머리말

<공무원> 영어 시험의 반 이상을 차지하는 독해의 중요성은 대부분의 수험생들이 잘 알고 있을 것이다. 그러나 그에 효과적으로 대비하는 방법을 정확히 알고 있는 경우는 드물다. 어휘를 열심히 외우고, 지문 속에서 답의 근거가 되는 문장이 어디인지 잘 파악하면 독해 문제는 자연스럽게 풀린다고 생각하는 경우가 많지만, 이는 잘못된 접근이다.

<독해> 실력을 키우는 데 있어 가장 기본적이고 중요한 전략은 문장을 정확히 읽어내는 힘을 기르는 것이다. 모든 글은 문단으로 이루어지기 이전에 개별 문장으로 구성된다. 익숙한 단어들만을 조합해 대충 뜻을 짐작하는 식의 독해는 결코 올바른 방법이 아니다.

<문장을> 정확히 이해하려면 어휘와 문법, 두 요소가 모두 탄탄해야 한다. 단어를 외울 때에는 가장 흔하게 쓰이는 첫 번째 뜻이 아니라, 배후에 숨겨진 다른 의미나 흔하게 쓰이는 덩어리까지 염두에 두어야 한다. 또 문장을 이해하려면 문장의 구조를 파악해야 하므로 문법 역시 중요하다. 문법 시간에 배운 이론을 실제 문장에 적용해 보며, 문장을 객관적으로 다룰 수 있어야 한다. 어휘, 문법, 문장의 해석은 따로 떨어진 것이 아니다. 문장 안에서 어휘와 문법이 어떻게 작용하는지를 반복적으로 경험하고 익혀야 문장으로 이루어진 지문도 자연스럽게 읽을 수 있다.

<마지막 기본 영어 – 구문편>은 단어의 실질적인 활용법과 문장 구조 분석을 통해 정확한 해석 능력을 기르고, 독해의 기본기를 체계적으로 다지는 것을 목표로 한다. 수험생들이 반드시 익혀야 할 핵심 구문과 문장이 길어지는 주요 원인들을 패턴별로 연습할 수 있도록 다양한 예문을 구성했으며, 관련된 어휘와 문법 포인트도 함께 정리하였다. 이 교재를 통해 문장을 읽는 힘을 기르고, 영어에 대한 자신감을 키우기를 기대한다.

<인생이라는> 길에는 크고 작은 돌들이 놓여 있기 마련이다. 누군가는 그 돌을 보고 걸림돌이라고 하겠지만, 다른 누군가는 디딤돌이라고 할 것이다. 여러분의 수험 여정 속에서 이 책이 작지만 든든한 디딤돌이 되어주길 바란다.

김태운 드림

CONTENTS

이 책의 차례

김태은 영어
마지막 기본 영어구문

CHAPTER 01 긴 명사 파악하기 — 6
1. 명사와 명사를 후치수식 하는 덩어리 — 6
2. 명사 취급 — 30

CHAPTER 02 여러 가지 동사의 모습 파악하기 — 70
1. 자동사 — 72
2. 타동사 — 82
3. 시제 x 태 — 114

CHAPTER 03 And, Or, But은 묶거나 끊기 — 130

CHAPTER 04 전치사, 접속사 해석하기 — 140
1. 결과를 나타내는 접속사 — 140
2. 시간을 나타내는 전치사와 접속사 — 142
3. 양보나 대조를 나타내는 전치사와 접속사 — 144
4. 인과를 나타내는 전치사와 접속사 — 146
5. 조건을 나타내는 전치사와 접속사 — 148
6. 목적을 나타내는 접속사 — 150

CHAPTER 05 준동사 정복하기 — 154
1. 부정사의 여러 가지 형태 — 154
2. 부정사의 여러 가지 해석 — 158
3. 동명사의 여러 가지 형태 — 164
4. 분사구문 — 166

 김태은 영어

마지막 기본 영어구문

CHAPTER

01

긴 명사 파악하기

1. 명사와 명사를 후치수식 하는 덩어리
2. 명사 취급

긴 명사 파악하기

1 명사와 명사를 후치수식하는 덩어리

명사 뒤에 다음의 여덟 가지가 등장하면 (소괄호)로 묶어서 후치수식하여 읽어야 한다. 한국어는 대체로 전치수식 구조를 취하기 때문에 당장 머릿속에서 후치수식의 해석이 자연스럽게 되지 않는 것이 정상이겠지만, 연습을 통해서 차차 적응해 나가길 기대한다.

> **(1) 형용사**
> 형용사는 명사 앞에서 명사를 전치수식하는 것이 원칙이나, 형용사가 두 단어 이상의 덩어리로 묶여서 쓰일 때는 후치수식하게 된다.

001 Games successful in one country do not always sell well in another.

002 The police responsible for counterterrorism keep updating data.

003 There are warning signs easy to be ignored on cigarette packs.

004 The Festival helps us form a common culture crucial to members of the group.

005 All investigators should be evaluated in a manner appropriate to their accomplishments.

내 인생 마지막 기본 영어구문

001 Games successful in one country do not always sell well in another.

[해석] 한 나라에서 성공한 게임이 항상 다른 나라에서 잘 팔리는 것은 아니다.
[KILLER]
• another은 단독으로 쓰이기도 하고, 단수명사와 쓰이기도 한다.
• another 단수명사, other 복수명사

[VOCA]
sell well 잘 팔리다
successful 성공적인
successive 연속적인

002 The police responsible for counterterrorism keep updating data.

[해석] 테러 방지 대책에 대해 책임이 있는 경찰은 계속해서 정보를 업데이트 한다.
[KILLER]
keep Ving : 계속해서 ~하다

[VOCA]
responsible (for) ~에 책임이 있다
counterterrorism 테러 방지

003 There are warning signs easy to be ignored on cigarette packs.

[해석] 담배 갑에는 무시되기 쉬운 위험 신호가 있다.
[KILLER]
주어 자리에 Here, There이 있으면 동사는 뒤에 있는 명사에 수일치 된다.

[VOCA]
easy to V ~하기 쉬운

004 The Festival helps us form a common culture crucial to members of the group.

[해석] 이 축제는 우리가 단체의 구성원들에게 중요한 공통의 문화를 형성하도록 돕는다.
[KILLER]
help + 명사 + (to) V : (명사)가 (동사)하는 것을 돕다

[VOCA]
form 형성하다
common 일반적인, 공통의
crucial 중요한

005 All investigators should be evaluated in a manner appropriate to their accomplishments.

[해석] 모든 조사관들은 그들 직업의 성과에 적절한 방식으로 평가받아야 한다.
[KILLER]
타동사 evaluate 뒤에 목적어가 없어서 수동태로 쓰였다.

[VOCA]
evaluate 평가하다
in a manner ~한 방식으로
appropriate 적절한
accomplishment 업적, 공적, 성과, 달성

Chapter 01 긴 명사 파악하기

006 Einstein sought relentlessly for a theory capable of describing nature's forces within a single, all-encompassing, and coherent framework.

007 Our intuitions are supposed to handle problems deep in our evolutionary past, not the newer complexities of the modern world.

008 Although Kate had something important to do on Sunday, she decided to cancel her plans and help me.

009 We found nothing inherently wrong with sticking to what we have chosen before.

> (2) 전치사
> 여러 가지 전치사가 전명구 형태로 명사를 후치수식할 수 있다. 전치사의 의미를 덩어리에 잘 녹여서 해석하는 것이 중요하다.

010 The boxes on the table are vacant.

011 He is a man of great influence in the political field.

012 They didn't consider his asylum an issue of importance.

006 Einstein sought relentlessly for a theory capable of describing nature's forces within a single, all-encompassing, and coherent framework.

해석 Einstein은 하나의, 모든 것을 아우르는, 일관된 뼈대 속에서 자연의 힘을 묘사하는 것이 가능한 이론을 끊임없이 추구했다.
KILLER
be able to V = be capable of Ving : ~하는 것이 가능하다, ~할 능력이 있다

VOCA
seek for ~를 찾다, 추구하다
relentlessly 쉬지 않고, 끊임없이
coherent 일관성 있는, 일관된

---

007 Our intuitions are supposed to handle problems deep in our evolutionary past, not the newer complexities of the modern world.

해석 우리 직관력은 현대의 새로운 복잡한 문제들이 아니라, 진화와 관련된 과거 깊은 곳에 있는 문제들을 다루는 것으로 여겨진다.
KILLER
- be supposed to V : ~하기로 되어 있다
- 자동사 deal with, cope with = 타동사 handle : 다루다

VOCA
intuition 직감, 직관력
evolutionary past 진화해 온 과거
complexities 복잡한 문제

---

008 Although Kate had something important to do on Sunday, she decided to cancel her plans and help me.

해석 Kate는 일요일에 중요한 일이 있었음에도 불구하고, 계획을 취소하고 나를 돕기로 결심했다.
KILLER
부정대명사인 ~thing/body/one/where을 꾸미는 형용사는 후치수식을 해야 한다.

---

009 We found nothing inherently wrong with sticking to what we have chosen before.

해석 우리는 우리가 전에 선택했던 것을 고수하는 데에 있어서 본질적으로 잘못된 어떤 것도 찾지 못했다.
KILLER
[what + 불]이 명사로 쓰여 전치사 to의 목적어 기능을 한다.

VOCA
inherently 선천적으로, 본질적으로
stick to 고수하다

---

010 The boxes on the table are vacant.

해석 탁자 위에 있는 상자들은 비어있다.

VOCA
vacant 텅 빈

---

011 He is a man of great influence in the political field.

해석 그는 정치계에서는 굉장히 영향력 있는 사람이다.

VOCA
of influence 영향력 있는

---

012 They didn't consider his asylum an issue of importance.

해석 그들은 그의 망명을 중요한 이슈라고 고려하지 않았다.
KILLER
consider A (as) B : A를 B라고 간주하다, 고려하다

VOCA
asylum 망명
of importance 중요한

013 The idea of achieving national security through thorough armament is a disastrous illusion at the present state of military technique.

014 One major difference between living in the city and in the country is the degree of friendliness among residents.

015 Decisions on resource allocation for the coming quarter will have to be set aside until the director arrives from his business trip.

013 The idea of achieving national security through thorough armament is a disastrous illusion at the present state of military technique.

해석 철저한 무장을 통해 안보를 이루려는 생각은 현재의 군사적 기술 상태에서는 위험한 망상이다.

VOCA
national security 국가 안보
thorough 철저한
armament 무장
disastrous 위험한, 처참한
illusion 환상, 오해
at the present state 현재 상태에서

014 One major difference between living in the city and in the country is the degree of friendliness among residents.

해석 도시에서 사는 것과 시골에서 사는 것 사이의 주요한 차이점은 주민들 사이의 친근함의 정도이다.

VOCA
degree 정도, 온도, 각도, 학위

015 Decisions on resource allocation for the coming quarter will have to be set aside until the director arrives from his business trip.

해석 다음 분기 자원 배치에 대한 결정은 관리자가 출장에서 돌아올 때까지 보류되어야 할 것이다.

KILLER
- 조동사 두 개를 붙여서 쓸 수 없으므로 will must가 아니라 will have to가 옳다.
- 타동사인 set aside(보류하다)의 목적어가 없으므로 수동형으로 쓰였다.
- until이 시간접속사이므로 시조부현미 문법에 의해 arrives는 현재시제여야 한다.
- arrive는 자동사, reach는 타동사이다.

VOCA
decision 판단, 결정
resource allocation 자원분배
coming 다가오는(= next)
set aside (1) 챙겨두다, 확보하다, 비축하다
(2) 무시하다, 보류하다

GUIDE and WEAPON

1. 원칙적으로는 주어가 '명사① 전치사 명사②' 형태로 쓰였을 경우, 뒤에 있는 전치사+명사②는 전명구이므로 명사①이 주어 역할을 한다.
2. 주어가 '부분(some, all, most, 분수, %) of 명사' 형태일 경우, 뒤에 있는 명사가 주어 역할을 한다.
3. a lot of, lots of, plenty of, a number of, an amount of, a host of, hosts of는 '많은'이라는 형용사로, 뒤에 있는 명사가 주어 역할을 한다.
4. a series of(일련의), a handful of(약간의, 소수의), a variety of(다양한), a range of(다양한)도 마찬가지이다.

예 1 More frequent use of computers creates a serious danger to health.
컴퓨터의 더욱 빈번한 사용이 건강에 심각한 위험을 야기하고 있다.

예 2 Most of the internal organs in existence in animal and human physiology are controlled by metabolism.
동물과 인간의 생리 속에 존재하는 내부 장기들 중 대부분은 신진대사에 의해 통제된다.

예 3 A range of policies have been introduced aimed at curbing inflation.
인플레이션 억제를 겨냥한 다양한 정책들이 도입되어 왔다.

> **(3) 부정사**
> 부정사는 그 명칭에서 알 수 있듯, 역할이 하나로 고정되어 있지 않고 다양하다. 그 중 형용사 기능을 할 때에는 덩어리로 묶여서 뒤에서 명사를 꾸며주는 역할을 하게 된다.

016 The opportunity to do the right things is right before you.

017 Failure to comply with rules written above nullifies the approval.

018 When I feel lonely, I try to find a person to talk with.

019 We need a house to live in.

020 William is the first to help you finish this race.

021 He must be the last man to do things sloppily, since he is meticulous.

022 Rome's agricultural output could not provide enough energy to maintain its infrastructure and the welfare of its citizens.

내 인생 **마지막 기본 영어구문**

016   The opportunity to do the right things is right before you.

  해석   옳은 일을 할 기회가 바로 네 앞에 있다.

017   Failure to comply with rules written above nullifies the approval.

  해석   상기된 규칙을 따르는 것에 실패하는 것은 승인을 무효화시킨다.

VOCA
comply with 따르다, 순응하다
nullify 무효화하다
approval 승인, 인정, 찬성

018   When I feel lonely, I try to find a person to talk with.

  해석   외롭다고 느낄 때, 나는 함께 이야기 할 사람을 찾으려 노력한다.
  KILLER
  talk가 자동사이므로 전치사 with가 필요하다.

019   We need a house to live in.

  해석   우리는 들어가서 살 집이 필요하다.
  KILLER
  live가 자동사이므로 전치사 in이 필요하다.

020   William is the first to help you finish this race.

  해석   William은 네가 이 경주를 끝낼 수 있도록 도울 첫 번째 사람임에 틀림없다. (분명히 도울 것이다.)
  KILLER
  the first (man) to V : 분명히 ~할 사람

021   He must be the last man to do things sloppily, since he is meticulous.

  해석   그는 일을 엉성하게 할 마지막 사람임이 분명한데(절대로 엉성하게 하지 않을 텐데), 그는 매우 꼼꼼하기 때문이다.
  KILLER
  the last (man) to V : 절대로 ~하지 않을 사람

VOCA
sloppily 대충, 엉성하게
meticulous 꼼꼼한

022   Rome's agricultural output could not provide enough energy to maintain its infrastructure and the welfare of its citizens.

  해석   로마의 농업생산량은 기반시설과 시민들의 복지를 유지할 정도로 충분한 에너지를 제공할 수 없었다.
  KILLER
  enough 명사 to V : (동사)할 정도로 충분한 (명사) (= 명사 enough to V)

VOCA
output 생산량
infrastructure 기반시설
welfare 복지

Chapter 01 긴 명사 파악하기   **13**

023 Character implies the ability to laugh wholeheartedly and weep unashamedly.

024 The capacity to store and distribute information has increased through the use of computers and other devices.

025 The failure of the family to experience their grief and pain together only perpetuates further mis-communication and alienation.

> **(4) 현재분사**
> 능동의 현재분사(Ving)는 한 단어일 때엔 명사 앞에서 전치수식하고, 두 단어 이상의 덩어리로 쓰인다면 후치수식해야 한다.

026 People living in a large city are often troubled by noise.

027 Researchers discussed two mobile phone companies trying to solve technological problems.

028 Anyone having difficulty in assembling the machine may take advantage of advice from our experts.

029 They adopted a curriculum consisting of liberal arts and natural sciences.

023 Character implies the ability to laugh wholeheartedly and weep unashamedly.

[해석] 인격은 마음껏 웃고 부끄럼 없이 울 수 있는 능력을 의미한다.

VOCA
imply 암시하다, 의미하다
wholeheartedly 진심으로, 마음껏
weep 울다, 훌쩍이다
unashamedly 부끄러워하지 않고, 뻔뻔하게

024 The capacity to store and distribute information has increased through the use of computers and other devices.

[해석] 정보를 저장하고 보급하는 능력이 컴퓨터와 다른 장치들의 사용을 통해 증가해 왔다.

[KILLER]
another + 단수명사, other + 복수명사

VOCA
capacity 능력, 용량
store 저장하다
distribute 보급하다, 전파하다
device 장치, 기구
devise 고안하다

025 The failure of the family to experience their grief and pain together only perpetuates further mis-communication and alienation.

[해석] 가족들이 그들의 슬픔과 고통을 함께하지 못하는 것은 오해와 고립을 계속해서 지속화시키기만 한다.

VOCA
grief 슬픔
perpetuate 영원하게 만든다
mis-communication 불통, 오해
alienation 고립

026 People living in a large city are often troubled by noise.

[해석] 대도시에 사는 사람들은 종종 소음 때문에 문제를 겪는다.

VOCA
be troubled by ~라는 문제를 겪는다, ~때문에 고생한다

027 Researchers discussed two mobile phone companies trying to solve technological problems.

[해석] 연구진들은 기술적 문제를 해결하려 노력하는 두 개의 휴대전화 회사에 대해 토론했다.

[KILLER]
discuss는 타동사이므로 명사인 목적어를 필요로 한다.

028 Anyone having difficulty in assembling the machine may take advantage of advice from our experts.

[해석] 기계를 조립하는 데 있어 어려움이 있는 사람이라면 누구든 우리 전문가의 조언을 이용할 수 있다.

[KILLER]
advice는 불가산명사이므로 복수형으로 쓸 수 없다.

VOCA
assemble 모으다, 조립하다
take advantage of 이용하다, 활용하다

029 They adopted a curriculum consisting of liberal arts and natural sciences.

[해석] 그들은 문과와 이과로 구성된 학습 계획을 채택했다.

[KILLER]
consist는 자동사이다.

VOCA
adopt 채택하다, 입양하다
adapt 조정/조절하다, 각색하다
consist of ~로 구성되다
liberal arts 문과, 교양과목
natural sciences 이과, 자연과학

030 There are 6 tons of trash including toxic metals and involving a variety of health hazards.

031 Doctors got more and more puzzled by new kinds of sickness appearing among their patients.

032 The International Monetary Fund (IMF) said that economic trouble affecting Asian countries would get better by the first half of 2009.

033 The number of people attending the trial was smaller than we had expected.

> **(5) 과거분사**
> 수동의 과거분사(p.p)는 한 단어일 때엔 명사 앞에서 전치수식하고, 두 단어 이상의 덩어리로 쓰인다면 후치수식해야 한다.

034 Poison used in a proper quantity will be a medicine.

035 Ninety percent of information stored in computers is in English.

036 I completed the test within the time allotted.

030 There are 6 tons of trash including toxic metals and involving a variety of health hazards.

해석 : 유해 금속을 포함하고 다양한 건강에 해로운 것들을 수반하는 쓰레기 6톤이 있다.
KILLER
trash는 불가산 명사이다.

VOCA
a variety of 다양한
hazard 해로움, 위협

031 Doctors got more and more puzzled by new kinds of sickness appearing among their patients.

해석 : 의사들은 그들의 환자 사이에서 발생하는 새로운 종류의 질환 때문에 점점 더 어리둥절해 했다.
KILLER
- 감정분사 puzzled는 doctors를 수식한다.
- appear은 자동사이다. '등장하다'라고 해석될 때엔 1형식, '~하게 보이다'라고 해석될 때엔 2형식으로 쓴다.

VOCA
puzzled 어리둥절한, 당황한
appear 등장하다, ~하게 보이다

032 The International Monetary Fund (IMF) said that economic trouble affecting Asian countries would get better by the first half of 2009.

해석 : 국제 통화 기금(IMF)은 아시아 국가들에 영향을 주고 있는 경제적 고통이 2009년 상반기까지는 좋아질 것이라고 말했다.
KILLER
- affect는 타동사로 '영향을 미치다', effect는 명사로 '영향, 결과'라는 뜻을 갖는다.
- by가 기한이나 시점과 함께 쓰이면 '~까지, ~무렵'이라고 해석한다.

VOCA
get better 나아지다
the first half 상반기, 전반
the last half 하반기, 후반

033 The number of people attending the trial was smaller than we had expected.

해석 : 재판에 참석한 사람들의 수는 우리가 예상했던 것보다 적었다.
KILLER
- the number of 복수명사 + 단수동사 : ~의 수
- attend가 '참석하다'라는 뜻일 경우 타동사로 쓴다.
- 비교급 smaller 이하에는 than(~보다)을 통해 비교 대상을 나타낸다.

VOCA
trial 재판, 시도, 실험
trial and error 시행착오

034 Poison used in a proper quantity will be a medicine.

해석 : 적정한 양으로 사용된 독은 약이 될 수 있다.

VOCA
quantity 양

035 Ninety percent of information stored in computers is in English.

해석 : 컴퓨터에 저장된 정보의 90%는 영어로 되어있다.
KILLER
주어가 '퍼센트(%) of 명사'이면 뒤에 있는 명사(information)가 주어 역할을 한다.

036 I completed the test within the time allotted.

해석 : 할당된 시간 내에 시험을 마쳤다.

VOCA
allot 분배하다, 할당하다

037 Huge quantities of carbon dioxide and methane released in the atmosphere have trapped heat and raised global temperature.

038 A black lawyer named Norah Gorman decided to take your case to the Supreme Court.

039 This pill belongs to a group of medicines known as "hypnotics." There are many different medicines of this type available to help people who suffer from insomnia. Insomnia is often transient and sporadic.

040 A helicopter piloted by an anonymous woman lifted a prisoner from a rooftop of La Sante Prison in Paris on Monday and flew him out.

041 The most remarkable substance in the world may probably be the element radium discovered by Marie and Pierre Curie.

042 One of the causes is our stubborn dependence on cars powered by fossil fuels.

043 The existing approaches may work well for problems that are similar to those previously solved.

037 Huge quantities of carbon dioxide and methane released in the atmosphere have trapped heat and raised global temperature.

[해석] 대기에 방출된 대량의 이산화탄소와 메탄은 열을 가두고 지구의 온도를 상승시켰다.
[KILLER]
rise는 자동사, raise는 타동사이다.

VOCA
release 방출/배출하다
atmosphere 대기, 분위기
trap 가두다

038 A black lawyer named Norah Gorman decided to take your case to the Supreme Court.

[해석] Norah Gorman이라는 이름의 한 흑인 변호사가 네 사건을 대법원으로 가져가기로 결심했다.

VOCA
case 사건
the Supreme Court 대법원

039 This pill belongs to a group of medicines known as "hypnotics." There are many different medicines of this type available to help people who suffer from insomnia. Insomnia is often transient and sporadic.

[해석] 이 약은 수면제로 알려진 약에 속한다. 불면증에 시달리는 사람들을 돕는 데 이용 가능한 많은 다른 종류의 약이 있다. 불면증은 종종 일시적이고 간헐적이다.

VOCA
belong to ~에 속하다
hypnotic 수면제
suffer from ~에 시달리다
insomnia 불면증
transient 일시적인
sporadic 간헐적인

040 A helicopter piloted by an anonymous woman lifted a prisoner from a rooftop of La Sante Prison in Paris on Monday and flew him out.

[해석] 한 익명의 여성에 의해 조종된 헬리콥터가 파리에서 월요일 La Sante 감옥의 지붕으로부터 한 수감자를 들어 올려 그를 비행기로 탈옥시켰다.
[KILLER]
문장의 동사가 lifted, flew로 두 개이다.

VOCA
pilot 조종하다
lift 들어 올리다
anonymous 익명의
unanimous 만장일치의

041 The most remarkable substance in the world may probably be the element radium discovered by Marie and Pierre Curie.

[해석] 아마도 세상에서 가장 주목할 만한 물질은 퀴리 부부에 의해 발견된 라듐 성분일 것이다.

VOCA
remarkable 눈에 띄는, 뛰어난, 주목할 만한
substance 물질

042 One of the causes is our stubborn dependence on cars powered by fossil fuels.

[해석] 원인 중의 하나는 화석 연료로 움직이는 차에 대한 우리의 완고한 의존이다.
[KILLER]
one of 복수명사 + 단수동사

VOCA
stubborn 완고한, 완강한
dependence 의존
power 동력을 공급하다, 작동시키다
fossil fuel 화석 연료

043 The existing approaches may work well for problems that are similar to those previously solved.

[해석] 기존의 접근법은 이전에 해결되었던 것들과 유사한 문제에 잘 작동할지도 모른다.
[KILLER]
• those는 problems를 가리키는 복수대명사이다.
• those를 수식하는 과거분사 solved는, 부사의 수식을 받으므로 previously가 옳다.

VOCA
existing 기존의
approach 접근 방법

> **(6) 관계사**
> 관계사는 불완전한 문장과 결합하는 관계대명사와, 완전한 문장과 결합하는 관계부사로 나누어진다. 관계사가 이끄는 문장의 범위를 정확하게 파악하여 괄호로 묶는 연습이 중요하다.

044 Motorists who have no regard for the safety of others ought to be punished.

045 Some of the laws that are supposed to protect innocent drivers from the consequences of hazardous driving habits are actually encouraging reckless driving.

046 Those who cannot make fruits out of their work or profession are usually ones whose concentration is poor.

047 Life is a game where there are multiple winners.

048 The day will never come when we will be free from troubles or wars.

049 There is little correlation between the situation that you are concerned about and the occurrence of the event that you fear.

044 Motorists who have no regard for the safety of others ought to be punished.

해석: 다른 사람의 안전을 고려하지 않는 운전자들은 당연히 처벌을 받게 된다.
KILLER
- ought to는 should와 같은 의미의 조동사이다.
- 타동사 punish가 목적어 없이 쓰였으므로 수동태가 적절하다.

VOCA
have a regard for ~를 고려하다, 배려하다
others 다른 사람들(= other people)

045 Some of the laws that are supposed to protect innocent drivers from the consequences of hazardous driving habits are actually encouraging reckless driving.

해석: 위험한 운전 습관의 결과로부터 잘못 없는 운전자들을 보호할 의무가 있는 법들 중 일부는 사실 난폭 운전을 부추기고 있다.
KILLER
주어가 'some of 명사' 형태이기 때문에 뒤에 있는 명사인 the laws가 주어 역할을 한다.

VOCA
protect A from B B로부터 A를 보호하다
innocent 순진한, 죄 없는, 무고한
consequence 결과
hazardous 위험한
encourage 부추기다, 격려하다
reckless driving 난폭운전

046 Those who cannot make fruits out of their work or profession are usually ones whose concentration is poor.

해석: 그들의 일이나 직업으로부터 성과를 낼 수 없는 사람들은 보통 집중력이 형편없는 이들이다.
KILLER
- those who ~ : ~한 사람들 (복수취급)
- out of = from : ~로부터

VOCA
fruit 성과, 실적
profession 직업

047 Life is a game where there are multiple winners.

해석: 인생은 다수의 승자가 있는 게임이다.

VOCA
multiple 많은, 다수의

048 The day will never come when we will be free from troubles or wars.

해석: 우리가 걱정이나 전쟁으로부터 자유로워지는 날은 절대 오지 않을 것이다.
KILLER
- 관계부사 when의 선행사는 the day이다. 관계사는 멀리 떨어진 선행사도 수식할 수 있다.
- 여기에서 when은 종속접속사가 아니므로 시조부현미의 수식을 받지 않기 때문에 we will be free 처럼 미래시제를 쓸 수 있다.

VOCA
be free from ~로부터 자유로워지다

049 There is little correlation between the situation that you are concerned about and the occurrence of the event that you fear.

해석: 당신이 걱정하고 있는 상황과 당신이 두려워하는 일의 발생 사이에는 상관관계가 없다.
KILLER
- between A and B : A와 B 사이에
- fear가 타동사로 쓰였다.

VOCA
correlation 연관
be concerned about ~를 걱정하다
be concerned with ~와 관련 있다
occurrence 발생
fear 두려워하다

050 The group to which I belong encourages individuals to think creatively.

051 Euthanasia is a legal, medical and ethical issue over which opinions diverge.

052 The authors understood that all humans carry distinctive mutations, which are not present in chimpanzees.

053 The grapes must be left on the vines until the first frost, after which they are harvested.

> ⑺ S + V
> 명사 뒤에 문장(S + V) 구조가 등장하는 경우가 있다. 이때엔 문장(S + V) 앞에 목적격 관계대명사 또는 관계부사가 생략되었다는 뜻이므로 역시 후치수식 구조로 파악하여 해석한다.

054 The house that they lived in is burning down.
= The house they lived in is burning down.

055 The reason why I don't want to go there is that I don't have enough money.
= Why I don't want to go there is that I don't have enough money.
= The reason I don't want to go there is that I don't have enough money.

056 He took the medicine the doctor prescribed.

050 The group to which I belong encourages individuals to think creatively.

> 해석 내가 속해 있는 집단은 개인 회원들이 창조적으로 생각하도록 격려한다.
> KILLER
> - which 뒤에는 불완전한 문장이 오지만, 전치사+which 뒤에는 완벽한 문장이 온다.
> - belong은 자동사이므로 I belong은 완벽한 문장이 맞다.
> - encourage A to V : A가 V하도록 부추기다, 격려하다

051 Euthanasia is a legal, medical and ethical issue over which opinions diverge.

> 해석 안락사는 의견이 갈라지는 법적, 의학적, 그리고 윤리적인 문제이다.
> KILLER
> diverge는 자동사로 '다양하게 갈라지다'라는 의미이다. 따라서 opinions diverge는 완벽한 문장으로 본다.

VOCA
euthanasia 안락사(= mercy killing)
diverge 갈라지다, 나뉘다, 벗어나다

052 The authors understood that all humans carry distinctive mutations, which are not present in chimpanzees.

> 해석 저자들은 모든 인간들이 침팬지들에게는 존재하지 않는 독특한 변이를 가지고 있다는 것을 이해했다.

VOCA
carry 운반하다, 지니다
distinctive 독특한
mutation 돌연변이, 변형, 변이
present (1) 선물
(2) 제시하다
(3) 존재하는, 참석한

053 The grapes must be left on the vines until the first frost, after which they are harvested.

> 해석 포도는 첫 서리 때까지 포도나무에 그대로 두어야 하며 그 후에 수확된다.

VOCA
vine 포도나무, 덩굴
the first frost 첫 서리
harvest 수확하다

054 The house that they lived in is burning down.
= The house they lived in is burning down.

> 해석 그들이 살았던 집이 불에 타고 있다.
> KILLER
> 목적격 관계대명사는 생략 가능하다.

055 The reason why I don't want to go there is that I don't have enough money.
= Why I don't want to go there is that I don't have enough money.
= The reason I don't want to go there is that I don't have enough money.

> 해석 내가 그곳에 가고 싶지 않은 이유는 돈이 충분히 없다는 것이다.
> KILLER
> 관계부사와 선행사는 둘 중 하나를 생략할 수 있다.

056 He took the medicine the doctor prescribed.

> 해석 그는 의사가 처방한 약을 먹었다.

VOCA
prescribe 처방하다

057 If an explosion occurs on a star, scientists on the earth will record the time it happened.

058 If you are accustomed to the noises cars are making, you will be startled by the silence of a town where only boats go by.

059 The pain and difficulties we face make us stronger and more competitive than comfort and ease.

060 Social scientists, teachers, and parents are troubled by the kinds of television programs children choose to watch.

061 The books children meet at school are the ones which have the greatest influence on their lives.

057 If an explosion occurs on a star, scientists on the earth will record the time it happened.

[해석] 만약 어떤 별에서 폭발이 발생하면, 지구에 있는 과학자들은 그것이 발생한 시간을 기록할 것이다.

[KILLER]
- if는 조건접속사이므로 시조부현미 문법에 의해 occurs는 현재형이어야 한다.
- the time 뒤에는 관계부사 when이 생략되어 있다.

[VOCA]
explosion 폭발, 폭파

058 If you are accustomed to the noises cars are making, you will be startled by the silence of a town where only boats go by.

[해석] 만약 네가 차가 만드는 소음에 익숙하다면, 오직 보트들만이 다니는 동네의 조용함에 놀랄 것이다.

[KILLER]
- be accustomed(= used) to 명사/Ving : ~에 익숙해지다
- if는 조건접속사이므로 시조부현미 문법에 의해 are 자리에는 will be가 불가능하다.
- 감정분사 startled가 you를 수식한다.
- go by (지나가다)는 자동사인 숙어이므로 boats go by는 완벽한 문장으로 보아야 한다.

[VOCA]
startled 깜짝 놀란
go by 지나가다, 흐르다

059 The pain and difficulties we face make us stronger and more competitive than comfort and ease.

[해석] 편하고 쉬운 것보다는 우리가 마주치는 고통이나 어려움이 우리를 더 강하고 능력 있게 만들어 준다.

[KILLER]
make + 명사 + 형용사 : (명사)를 (형용사)하게 만들다

[VOCA]
competitive 경쟁력 있는, 뛰어난
comfort 안락함, 위로
ease 쉬움, 편안함

060 Social scientists, teachers, and parents are troubled by the kinds of television programs children choose to watch.

[해석] 사회학자, 교사 및 부모님은 어린이들이 시청하겠다고 선택한 TV 프로그램의 종류 때문에 곤란을 겪는다.

[KILLER]
choose는 부정사를 목적어로 취하는 3형식 동사이다.

061 The books children meet at school are the ones which have the greatest influence on their lives.

[해석] 아이들이 학교에서 접하는 책들은 아마도 그들의 삶에 가장 큰 영향을 주는 책이 될 것이다.

[KILLER]
주격 관계대명사 which 이하에는 선행사 the ones에 수일치된 복수동사 have가 적절하다.

> **(8) 동격**
> 동격이란 어떤 명사를 보충 설명하기 위해 다른 명사를 연달아 붙여서 설명하는 것을 이야기 하는데, 동격을 표현하는 방법은 생각보다 다양하다.

062 A lion, one of the most dangerous animals, was awakened from sleep by a mouse running over his face.

063 He began to realize that Newton's theory of gravitation, the unchallenged law, contained serious problems.

064 The news of her marriage is not true.

065 I can't believe the fact of your meeting her.

066 One argument for permitting the buying and selling of kidneys rests on the libertarian notion of self-ownership: If I own my own body, I should be free to sell my body parts as I please.

067 We all are aware of the fact that all humans are mortal.

062 A lion, one of the most dangerous animals, was awakened from sleep by a mouse running over his face.

[해석] 가장 위험한 동물들 중 하나인 사자가 그의 얼굴 위를 달려서 지나가는 쥐 때문에 잠에서 깨어났다.

KILLER
- one of 복수명사 : ~중 하나
- awaken(깨우다)은 타동사이다. be awaken from sleep by(~때문에 잠에서 깨다) 형태로 자주 쓰인다.

063 He began to realize that Newton's theory of gravitation, the unchallenged law, contained serious problems.

[해석] 그는 이의가 제기되지 않은 법칙인 뉴턴의 중력 이론에 심각한 문제가 있다는 것을 깨닫기 시작했다.

VOCA
gravitation 중력
unchallenged 도전받지 않는, 확고한
contain (1) 포함하다, 가지다
(2) 억누르다, 억제하다

064 The news of her marriage is not true.

[해석] 그녀의 결혼이라는 소식은 진짜가 아니다.

KILLER
news는 불가산명사이므로 단수 취급한다.

065 I can't believe the fact of your meeting her.

[해석] 나는 네가 그를 만났다는 사실을 믿을 수 없다.

KILLER
동명사 앞에 소유격을 쓰면 의미상 주어가 된다.

066 One argument for permitting the buying and selling of kidneys rests on the libertarian notion of self-ownership: If I own my own body, I should be free to sell my body parts as I please.

[해석] 신장(콩팥)의 매매를 허용해야 한다는 주장 중 하나는 '자기 소유권'이라는 자유지상주의적 개념에 근거한다. 즉, 만약 내가 내 몸을 소유하고 있다면, 나는 내 몸의 일부를 내가 원하는 대로 팔 자유가 있어야 한다는 것이다.

KILLER
- be free to V : 자유롭게/마음껏 ~하다
- be free of N : ~가 없다, 들어있지 않다
- be free from N : ~가 없다, ~로부터 벗어나다

VOCA
argument 논쟁, 말다툼, 주장
kidney 신장, 콩팥
rest on ~에 달려있다, 기초하다, 근거하다
libertarian 자유지상주의적인
self-ownership 자기 소유권

067 We all are aware of the fact that all humans are mortal.

[해석] 우리 모두는 모든 인간이 죽을 것이라는 사실을 알고 있다.

KILLER
the fact that에서 that은 동격이므로 that 이하에 완전한 문장이 온다.

VOCA
be aware of ~를 알다, 인지하다
mortal (언젠가는) 죽을 운명의
immortal 불사의

068 The rumor is abroad that the police arrested smugglers.

069 The radio commentator announced the news that oil prices fluctuated.

068 The rumor is abroad that the police arrested smugglers.

해석 경찰이 밀수업자들을 체포했다는 소문이 퍼졌다.

069 The radio commentator announced the news that oil prices fluctuated.

해석 라디오 해설자는 유가가 급변했다는 뉴스를 발표했다.

VOCA
abroad (1) 해외로 (2) 널리 퍼져
smuggler 밀수업자
smuggle 밀수하다

VOCA
fluctuate 급변하다, 오르락내리락하다

2 명사 취급

영어의 명사 자리(주어, 목적어, 보어)에는 명사뿐만 아니라 명사 취급도 쓰일 수 있다.

> (1) 부정사
> - 부정사는 명사취급되는 덩어리이므로 문장의 주어, 목적어, 보어 자리에 종종 쓰인다.
> - 그러나 전치사의 목적어 자리에는 쓰일 수 없다.
> - 특히 가주어, 가목적어 it을 취하면서 부정사가 진주어, 진목적어로 쓰이는 구문은 자주 쓰이기도 하고 문법적으로도 중요하므로 유의하여 연습한다.

070 To know is one thing, and to teach is another.

071 To be a good friend is to offer true understanding at all times.

072 To remain courageous under all circumstances indicates strong self-confidence.

073 A good way to focus on your goals is to write them down.

074 To keep a balance between ends and means is both difficult and important.

075 To exclude those from voting who are already socially isolated destroys democracy.

070 To know is one thing, and to teach is another.

[해석] 아는 것과 가르치는 것은 별개이다.
KILLER
- 부정사 주어 (단수 취급)
- A is one thing, and B is another : A와 B는 별개이다

071 To be a good friend is to offer true understanding at all times.

[해석] 좋은 친구가 된다는 것은 항상 진짜 이해를 해 주는 것이다.
KILLER
부정사 주어, 부정사 보어

VOCA
at all times 계속, 끊임없이

072 To remain courageous under all circumstances indicates strong self-confidence.

[해석] 어떤 상황에서도 용감한 상태를 유지하는 것은 확고한 자신감을 나타낸다.
KILLER
- 부정사 주어 (단수 취급 indicates)
- 2형식 remain + 형용사

VOCA
under all circumstances 어떤 상황 하에서도, 항상
indicate 나타내다, 보여주다

073 A good way to focus on your goals is to write them down.

[해석] 당신의 목적에 집중하는 좋은 방법은 그것들을 적는 것이다.
KILLER
- 부정사 보어
- 대명사 목적어는 이어동사 사이에 위치해야 한다.

VOCA
write down (글로) 적다

074 To keep a balance between ends and means is both difficult and important.

[해석] 목적과 수단 사이에서 균형을 잡는 것은 어렵고 중요한 일이다.
KILLER
- 부정사 주어
- both A and B : A와 B 둘 다

VOCA
ends and means 목적과 수단

075 To exclude those from voting who are already socially isolated destroys democracy.

[해석] 이미 사회적으로 고립된 사람들을 투표로부터 배제하는 것은 민주주의를 파괴한다.
KILLER
- 부정사 주어 (단수 취급 destroys)
- exclude A from B : B로부터 A를 배제시키다
- those who ~ : ~한 사람들

VOCA
socially 사회적으로

076 There are times when you need to get directly to the core of an issue.

077 Often people don't want to be the first to comment on a controversial post.

078 Instead of putting more armed police in the street, they chose to play classical music.

079 Through his act he saved her life, yet he refused to receive praise.

080 It is critical in the A.I. age to acquire the habit of reading, and not to allow your mind to become lazy.

081 It is difficult for Americans to imagine a life arranged according to the Korean pattern.

076 There are times when you need to get directly to the core of an issue.

> 해석 : 문제의 핵심에 직접 접근해야 할 필요가 있는 시기가 있다.
> KILLER
> • 부정사 목적어 (need to V: ~할 필요가 있다)
> • Here/There로 시작하는 문장의 동사는 뒤에 있는 명사에 수일치를 시킨다.

VOCA
get to ~에 닿다, 도착하다

077 Often people don't want to be the first to comment on a controversial post.

> 해석 : 종종 사람들은 논란이 많은 게시물에 댓글을 다는 첫 번째 사람이 되고 싶어 하지 않는다.
> KILLER
> • 부정사 목적어 (want to V: ~하고 싶다)
> • the first to V: ~할 첫 번째 사람

VOCA
comment on ~를 논하다, 각주/댓글을 달다
controversial 논란이 많은

078 Instead of putting more armed police in the street, they chose to play classical music.

> 해석 : 거리에 더 많은 무장 경찰을 배치하는 대신, 그들은 클래식 음악을 연주하는 것을 선택했다.
> KILLER
> • 부정사 목적어 (choose to V: ~를 선택하다)
> • 전치사(instead of)의 목적어는 동명사가 옳다.

VOCA
armed 무장한

079 Through his act he saved her life, yet he refused to receive praise.

> 해석 : 그는 자신의 행동을 통해 그녀의 생명을 구했지만, 칭찬을 받기를 거부했다.
> KILLER
> 부정사 목적어 (refuse to V: ~하기를 거부하다)

VOCA
praise 칭찬(하다)

080 It is critical in the A.I. age to acquire the habit of reading, and not to allow your mind to become lazy.

> 해석 : 인공지능 시대에서 독서하는 습관을 만들고 마음이 나태해지도록 허락하지 않는 것이 매우 중요하다.
> KILLER
> • 가주어-진주어(to V) 구문
> • 등위접속사 and는 두 개의 부정사를 병치시키고 있다.
> • 부정사를 부정하는 not은 앞에 둔다. (not to V)
> • 5형식 allow A to V: A가 V하도록 허락하다

VOCA
critical 매우 중요한
A.I. (Artificial Intelligence) 인공지능

081 It is difficult for Americans to imagine a life arranged according to the Korean pattern.

> 해석 : 미국인들이 한국식에 따라 짜여진 생활을 상상하는 것은 어려운 일이다.
> KILLER
> • 가주어-진주어(to V) 구문
> • 부정사의 의미상 주어는 전치사 for로 표현한다.

VOCA
arrange (일을) 처리하다, 배열하다, 마련하다, 일정을 짜다

082 I found it difficult to get along with Kate, possibly because of the age gap between us.

083 He asked a friend who works at the bank to make it possible for him to get a loan.

> (2) 동명사
> ― 동명사는 명사 취급되는 덩어리이므로 문장의 주어, 목적어, 보어 자리에 종종 쓰인다.
> ― 전치사의 목적어 자리에는 부정사가 아닌 동명사가 쓰여야 한다.

084 Calculating the number of people in large countries turns out to be not an easy job.

085 Making an effort to communicate in another person's language shows your respect for him.

086 Simply moving the patient to a bed that is near a window and darkening the room at night can significantly improve mental state.

082 I found it difficult to get along with Kate, possibly because of the age gap between us.

해석 나는 Kate와 잘 지내는 것을 어렵다고 생각했는데, 아마도 나이 차이 때문이었을 것이다.
KILLER
가목적어-진목적어(to get along) 구문

VOCA
get along with 친하게 지내다, 잘 지내다

083 He asked a friend who works at the bank to make it possible for him to get a loan.

해석 그는 은행에서 일하는 친구에게 대출을 받을 수 있게 해달라고 부탁했다.
KILLER
- 가목적어-진목적어(to get a loan) 구문
- 5형식 ask A to V : A가 V하도록 요청/요구/부탁하다
- 부정사의 의미상 주어는 전치사 for로 표현한다.

VOCA
get a loan 대출을 받다

084 Calculating the number of people in large countries turns out to be not an easy job.

해석 큰 나라의 인구수를 계산하는 것은 쉽지 않은 일로 드러났다.
KILLER
- 동명사 주어 (단수 취급 turns out)
- the number of 복수명사 (+ 단수동사) : ~의 수
- turn out (to be) 명사 또는 형용사 : ~인 것으로 드러나다

085 Making an effort to communicate in another person's language shows your respect for him.

해석 다른 사람의 언어로 의사소통하기 위해 노력하는 것은 그 사람에 대한 존중을 보여준다.
KILLER
- 동명사 주어 (단수 취급 shows)
- make an effort to V : ~하기 위해 노력하다

086 Simply moving the patient to a bed that is near a window and darkening the room at night can significantly improve mental state.

해석 단순히 환자를 창문 근처 침대로 옮기고 밤에 방을 어둡게 하는 것만으로도 정신 상태를 크게 개선할 수 있다.
KILLER
- 동명사 주어
- 등위접속사 and가 동명사 주어 두개를 병치시킨다.
- 주격 관계대명사 that은 수일치가 중요하다. 선행사인 a bed에 맞추어 이하엔 단수동사 is가 온다.

VOCA
darken 어둡게 하다
significantly 상당히, 매우
improve 개선시키다

087 Finding a misplaced remote control, smart-phone or car keys is not just an annoyance, but a time-consuming endeavor.

088 Avoid judging your own value by comparing yourself with others.

089 A Dutch auction starts with a high price that keeps going down until the item is sold.

090 Talking assertively does not necessarily mean feeling disagreeable.

091 People often don't consider taking care of the pool during the winter.

092 He came up with the creative idea of posting notes everywhere with the simple message.

087 Finding a misplaced remote control, smart-phone or car keys is not just an annoyance, but a time-consuming endeavor.

해석 없어진 리모컨, 스마트 폰 또는 자동차 키를 찾는 것은 성가신 일일 뿐만 아니라 시간이 많이 걸리는 노력이다.

KILLER
- 동명사 주어 (단수 취급 is)
- not only(= just) A but B : A뿐만 아니라 B도

VOCA
misplaced 어디에 있는지 모르는, 없어진
annoyance 성가신 일
time-consuming 시간이 걸리는
endeavor 노력

088 Avoid judging your own value by comparing yourself with others.

해석 자신을 다른 사람들과 비교함으로써 자신의 가치를 판단하지 말아라.

KILLER
- 동명사 목적어 (avoid Ving : ~하는 것을 피하다)
- 동명사는 전치사의 목적어 역할을 할 수 있다. (by Ving : ~함으로써)

089 A Dutch auction starts with a high price that keeps going down until the item is sold.

해석 네덜란드 경매는 물건이 팔릴 때까지 계속 내려가는 높은 가격으로 시작된다.

KILLER
- 동명사 목적어 (keep Ving : 계속해서 ~하다)
- that은 a high price를 수식하는 주격 관계대명사이다.

090 Talking assertively does not necessarily mean feeling disagreeable.

해석 단호하게 말하는 것이 반드시 불쾌하게 느낀다는 뜻은 아니다

KILLER
- 동명사 주어, 동명사 목적어 (mean Ving : ~를 뜻하다)
- not necessarily : 반드시 ~한 것은 아니다

VOCA
assertively 단호하게
disagreeable 불쾌한

091 People often don't consider taking care of the pool during the winter.

해석 사람들은 종종 겨울 동안 수영장을 돌보는 것을 고려하지 않는다.

KILLER
동명사 목적어 (consider Ving : ~를 고려하다, 고민하다)

VOCA
take care of 돌보다

092 He came up with the creative idea of posting notes everywhere with the simple message.

해석 그는 간단한 메시지를 담은 쪽지를 모든 곳에 게시하는 창의적인 아이디어를 떠올렸다.

KILLER
동명사는 전치사의 목적어 자리에 쓰일 수 있다.

VOCA
come up with 생각해내다, 떠올리다, 고안하다

> **(3) 명사절 접속사 that + 완벽한 문장**
> - [that + 완벽한 문장]은 한 덩어리의 명사 취급을 받기 때문에 주어, 목적어, 보어 자리에 자유롭게 들어갈 수 있다.
> - 특히 가주어, 가목적어 it을 취하면서 [that + 완]이 진주어, 진목적어로 쓰이는 구문은 자주 쓰이기도 하고 문법적으로도 중요하므로 유의하여 연습한다.
> - 타동사의 목적어로 쓰인 [that + 완]에서 that은 생략할 수 있다.

093 That the earth must be flat seemed obvious until the 15th century.
　　 = It seemed obvious until the 15th century that the earth must be flat.

094 That craze of the Korean wave has increased the number of tourists is great news.

095 It is not a new idea that cooking is an activity that defines humans.

096 It is rare that after the age of twelve a speaker will learn a new language without having at least a slight accent.

097 It is now commonly believed that birds use both the sun and their natural sense of time to migrate long distances.

098 Scientists once thought that we were the only intelligent life on this planet.

내 인생 마지막 기본 영어구문

093 That the earth must be flat seemed obvious until the 15th century.
= It seemed obvious until the 15th century that the earth must be flat.

[해석] 지구가 평평한 것이 분명하다는 것은 15세기까지 명백해 보였다.
KILLER
- [that + 완] 주어
- 2형식 seem + 형용사 obvious

VOCA
obvious 명백한, 분명한

094 That craze of the Korean wave has increased the number of tourists is great news.

[해석] 한류 열풍이 관광객의 수를 증가시켰다는 것은 좋은 소식이다.
KILLER
- [that + 완] 주어
- the number of 복수명사 : ~의 수

VOCA
craze 열광

095 It is not a new idea that cooking is an activity that defines humans.

[해석] 요리가 인간을 정의하는 활동이라는 것은 새로운 생각이 아니다.
KILLER
[that + 완] 진주어

096 It is rare that after the age of twelve a speaker will learn a new language without having at least a slight accent.

[해석] 12살 이후에 화자가 최소한 약간의 억양을 갖지 않고 새로운 언어를 배우는 것은 드문 일이다.
KILLER
- [that + 완] 진주어
- without Ving : ~하지 않고

097 It is now commonly believed that birds use both the sun and their natural sense of time to migrate long distances.

[해석] 새들은 먼 거리를 이동하기 위해 태양과 그들의 타고난 시간 감각을 모두 사용한다고 알려져 있다.
KILLER
- [that + 완] 진주어
- use A to V : V하기 위해 A(명사)를 이용/활용하다

VOCA
natural 타고난
migrate 이동하다, 이주하다

098 Scientists once thought that we were the only intelligent life on this planet.

[해석] 과학자들은 한때 우리가 지구에서의 유일한 지적 생명체라고 생각했다.
KILLER
[that + 완] 목적어 (생략 가능)

099 Researchers say that reality TV programs offer several benefits to consumers including satisfying their curiosity.

100 Some early childhood educators believe that in modern society computer skills are a basic necessity for every child.

101 The most common mistake made by amateur photographers is that they are not physically close enough to their subjects.

102 To suggest that narcissism is the predominant element underlying teenagers' interest in contemporary foreign books would be seriously misleading.

103 With all the passion for being slim, it is no wonder that many people view any amount of visible fat on the body as something to get rid of.

099 Researchers say that reality TV programs offer several benefits to consumers including satisfying their curiosity.

해석 연구원들은 리얼리티 TV 프로그램이 그들의 호기심을 만족시키는 것을 포함하여 소비자들에게 몇 가지 이점을 제공한다고 말한다.
KILLER
[that + 완] 목적어 (생략 가능)

VOCA
satisfy 충족시키다
curiosity 호기심

100 Some early childhood educators believe that in modern society computer skills are a basic necessity for every child.

해석 일부 유아 교육자들은 현대 사회에서 컴퓨터 기술은 모든 어린이들에게 필수 요소라고 믿는다.
KILLER
• [that + 완] 목적어 (생략 가능)
• every + 단수명사 (모든 ~)

VOCA
necessity 필수품, 필수 요소

101 The most common mistake made by amateur photographers is that they are not physically close enough to their subjects.

해석 아마추어 사진작가들이 저지르는 가장 흔한 실수는 피사체에 물리적으로 충분히 가까이 있지 않다는 것이다.
KILLER
[that + 완] 보어

VOCA
subject 주제, 과목, 피실험자, 피사체, 백성, 대상

102 To suggest that narcissism is the predominant element underlying teenagers' interest in contemporary foreign books would be seriously misleading.

해석 나르시시즘이 현대 외국 책에 대한 십대들의 관심의 근본적인 주요 요소라고 제안하는 것은 심각하게 오도될 것이다.
KILLER
[that + 완] 목적어 (생략 가능)

VOCA
predominant 두드러진, 우세한, 지배적인(= dominant)
interest 관심
underlying 근본적인 (underlie의 현재분사)
contemporary 현대의
misleading 잘못된, 오해의 소지가 있는

103 With all the passion for being slim, it is no wonder that many people view any amount of visible fat on the body as something to get rid of.

해석 날씬해지려는 그 모든 열정 때문에, 많은 사람들이 몸에 보이는 어떤 양의 지방도 없애야 할 것으로 간주하는 것은 당연한 일이다.
KILLER
• [that + 완] 진주어
• it is no wonder that : ~는 놀랄 일이 아니다, 당연한 일이다
• view A as B : A를 B라고 간주하다

VOCA
passion 열정
get rid of 없애다, 제거하다
(= dispose of, do away with, eliminate)

104 One of the most immediate benefits of a web-seminar is that it can eliminate a large portion of your company's travel budget.

105 A significant problem with alternative fuels made from crops is that they can decrease the supply of important foods.

106 But it seems likely that human beings who can put men on the moon and produce computers can bring off another miracle.

107 That consciousness of self and freedom go together is shown in the fact that the less self-awareness a person has, the more unfree he is.

---

(4) 관계대명사 what + 불완전한 문장
- [what + 불완전한 문장]은 한 덩어리의 명사 취급을 받기 때문에 주어, 목적어, 보어 자리에 자유롭게 들어갈 수 있다.
- 관계대명사 what은 선행사를 취할 수 없다는 점에 유의한다.
- what은 생략할 수 없다.

---

108 What is done cannot be undone.

109 What has been achieved in this field is very little.

104 One of the most immediate benefits of a web-seminar is that it can eliminate a large portion of your company's travel budget.

[해석] 웹 세미나의 가장 즉각적인 이점 중 하나는 회사 여행 예산의 많은 부분을 제거할 수 있다는 것이다.
KILLER
[that + 완] 보어

VOCA
immediate 즉각적인, 가까이에 있는
eliminate 없애다

105 A significant problem with alternative fuels made from crops is that they can decrease the supply of important foods.

[해석] 농작물로부터 만들어지는 대체 연료의 중요한 문제는 그것들이 중요한 식량의 공급을 감소시킬 수 있다는 것이다.
KILLER
[that + 완] 보어

VOCA
significant 중요한
alternative fuel 대체 연료
↔ fossil fuel 화석 연료
 (coal 석탄 + oil 석유)

106 But it seems likely that human beings who can put men on the moon and produce computers can bring off another miracle.

[해석] 달에도 갈 수 있고 컴퓨터도 만들 수 있는 인간은 또 다른 기적도 이루어낼 수 있을 것 같다.
KILLER
• [that + 완] 진주어
• it is(= seems) likely that ~ : ~할 가능성이 높다, ~할 것 같다

VOCA
likely 가능성이 높은
bring off 훌륭히 해내다, 성취하다

107 That consciousness of self and freedom go together is shown in the fact that the less self-awareness a person has, the more unfree he is.

[해석] 자아의식과 자유가 함께 공존한다는 것은 자기인식이 덜한 사람일수록 더욱 자유롭지 못하다는 사실에서 나타난다.
KILLER
• [that + 완] 주어
• the 비교급 ~, the 비교급 ~ : ~할수록 ~하다

VOCA
consciousness of self 자아의식
go together 함께 가다, 공존하다
self-awareness 자기 인식

108 What is done cannot be undone.

[해석] 끝난 일은 취소할 수 없다.
KILLER
[what + 불] 주어

109 What has been achieved in this field is very little.

[해석] 이 분야에서 달성된 것은 거의 없다.
KILLER
[what + 불] 주어 (단수 취급 is)

110 What Chris did instead was insidious.

111 What offended me at the previous meeting was his discourteous remarks.

112 What you do in the 15 to 30 minutes after eating meals sends your metabolism powerful signals.

113 What we have to be careful about is that the internet has a totally undeserved instant credibility.

114 The young generation has gone beyond what their antecedents had promised.

115 There is no clear dividing line between what is good and what is bad.

110 What Chris did instead was insidious.

[해석] Chris가 그 대신에 한 것은 교활했다.
[KILLER]
[what + 불] 주어 (단수 취급 was)

VOCA
insidious 교활한

111 What offended me at the previous meeting was his discourteous remarks.

[해석] 지난 미팅에서 나를 불쾌하게 했던 것은 그의 무례한 발언들이었다.
[KILLER]
[what + 불] 주어 (단수 취급 was)

VOCA
offend (1) (범죄를) 저지르다
       (2) (사람을) 불쾌하게 하다
discourteous 예의 없는, 무례한

112 What you do in the 15 to 30 minutes after eating meals sends your metabolism powerful signals.

[해석] 식사를 하고 난 뒤 15분에서 30분 동안 하는 것이 당신의 신진대사에 강력한 신호를 보낸다.
[KILLER]
[what + 불] 주어 (단수 취급 sends)

113 What we have to be careful about is that the internet has a totally undeserved instant credibility.

[해석] 우리가 조심해야 할 점은 그것이 완전히 부당한 즉각적인 신뢰성을 가지고 있다는 것이다.
[KILLER]
[what + 불] 주어 (단수 취급 is)

VOCA
totally 완전히
undeserved 받을 만하지 않은,
           받을 자격이 없는,
           부당한, 과분한
instant 즉각적인
credibility 신뢰성

114 The young generation has gone beyond what their antecedents had promised.

[해석] 젊은 세대는 그들의 선조들이 약속했던 것을 넘어섰다.
[KILLER]
• [what + 불] 전치사의 목적어
• [that + 완]은 전치사의 목적어 자리에 쓰일 수 없다.

VOCA
go beyond ~를 초월하다,
          ~를 넘어서다
antecedent 선조, 조상

115 There is no clear dividing line between what is good and what is bad.

[해석] 좋은 것과 나쁜 것 사이에 분명한 경계선은 없다.
[KILLER]
[what + 불] 전치사의 목적어

VOCA
dividing line 경계선, 구분선

116 You will make fewer mistakes in life by paying attention to what others are doing than by neglecting it.

117 Dexter, a stranger in the land, found it very difficult to figure out what to do.

118 The nurses, the medical students and the theology students were deeply interested in the method for nobody had ever taught them what they should learn to help dying patients.

119 Numerous surveys have repeatedly shown that the belief that fate or luck significantly determines what happens in one's life is not influential among Americans.

120 I don't know what subject I want to major in or what kind of job I want to get.

116 You will make fewer mistakes in life by paying attention to <u>what others are doing</u> than by neglecting it.

[해석] 남들이 무엇을 하는가를 무시하기보다는 그것에 주의를 기울임으로써, 인생에서 더 적은 잘못을 저지르게 될 것이다.

[KILLER]
- [what + 불] 전치사의 목적어
- by Ving : ~함으로써

[VOCA]
pay attention to ~에 집중하다, 주의하다
neglect 무시하다

117 Dexter, a stranger in the land, found it very difficult to figure out <u>what to do</u>.

[해석] 이 땅에 처음 온 Dexter는 무엇을 해야 할지 파악하는 것이 매우 어렵다고 생각했다.

[KILLER]
- what to V : 무엇을 V해야 할지
- find it 형용사 to V (가목적어 it – 진목적어 to V 구문)

[VOCA]
figure out 파악하다

118 The nurses, the medical students and the theology students were deeply interested in the method for nobody had ever taught them <u>what they should learn to help dying patients</u>.

[해석] 간호사와 의대생, 신학생들은 그들에게 죽어가는 환자를 돕기 위해 무엇을 배워야 할지 가르쳐준 사람이 없었기 때문에, 그 방식에 매우 깊은 흥미를 보였다.

[KILLER]
- [what + 불] 4형식 teach의 직접목적어
- 접속사 for : ~하기 때문에(= because)

[VOCA]
medical student 의대생
theology student 신학생
be interested in ~에 흥미가 있다
patient 환자

119 Numerous surveys have repeatedly shown that the belief that fate or luck significantly determines <u>what happens in one's life</u> is not influential among Americans.

[해석] 수많은 조사결과는 운이나 행운이 일생에서 발생하는 것을 상당히 결정한다는 믿음이 미국인 사이에서는 별로 영향력이 없다는 점을 반복적으로 보여주었다.

[KILLER]
- [what + 불] 목적어
- the belief that ~에서 that은 동격
- determine N (~를 결정하다) vs. be determined to V (~하기로 결심하다)

[VOCA]
numerous 수많은
repeatedly 여러 차례
fate 운명
significantly 상당히
influential 영향력 있는

120 I don't know <u>what subject I want to major in</u> or <u>what kind of job I want to get</u>.

[해석] 나는 내가 어떤 과목을 전공하고 싶은지 또는 어떤 종류의 직업을 갖길 원하는지를 잘 모르겠다.

[KILLER]
what 명사 S + V : 어떤 (명사)를 S가 V하는지

[VOCA]
major in 전공하다

121 She didn't know what type or size she needed, so I asked her what kind of car she had.

122 In the field of science, finding out what does not work is as important as finding out what does.

123 Because the new law regulates what has long been regarded as conventional practices, officials are concerned about what they are doing.

124 They protect themselves by what is called protective coloring.

125 Reading is to the mind what exercise is to the body.

126 What is worse, assistant managers seem not to know how to solve the problem.

121 She didn't know what type or size she needed, so I asked her what kind of car she had.

[해석] 그녀는 어떤 종류나 사이즈를 그녀가 원하는지 알지 못했고, 그래서 나는 그녀에게 어떤 종류의 차를 그녀가 가지고 있는지를 물었다.

122 In the field of science, finding out what does not work is as important as finding out what does.

[해석] 과학이라는 영역에서는, 잘 되지 않는 것을 알아내는 것이 잘 되는 것을 알아내는 것만큼 중요하다.

KILLER
• [what + 불] 목적어
• 대동사 does(= does work)

123 Because the new law regulates what has long been regarded as conventional practices, officials are concerned about what they are doing.

[해석] 새로운 법률은 오랫동안 관례적인 관습으로 간주되었던 것을 규제하기 때문에, 공무원들은 그들의 행동에 대해 걱정한다.

KILLER
[what + 불] 목적어

124 They protect themselves by what is called protective coloring.

[해석] 그들은 이른바 보호색이라고 하는 것으로 스스로를 방어한다.

KILLER
• what is called : 소위 ~, 이른바 ~
• 주어와 목적어가 같을 때에는, 목적어 자리에 재귀대명사(~self, 스스로)를 써야 한다.

125 Reading is to the mind what exercise is to the body.

[해석] 독서와 정신의 관계는 운동과 신체의 관계와 같다.

KILLER
A is to B what C is to D : A와 B의 관계는 C와 D의 관계와 같다.

126 What is worse, assistant managers seem not to know how to solve the problem.

[해석] 설상가상으로 대리들조차 그 문제를 어떻게 해결해야 할지 알지 못하는 것처럼 보인다.

KILLER
• what is worse : 설상가상으로
• seem to V : V인 것처럼 보인다
• how to V : 어떻게 V해야 할지

VOCA
regulate 규제하다
regard A as B A를 B라고 간주하다
conventional practice 관습
official 공무원
be concerned about 걱정하다

(5) whether과 if 명사절
- whether과 if 명사절은 둘 다 '~인지 아닌지', '~인지의 여부'라고 해석이 된다.
- [whether S + V] 명사절은 주어, 목적어, 보어 자리에 쓰일 수 있다.
- [if S + V] 명사절은 타동사의 목적어 자리와 진주어에만 쓰일 수 있다.
- 문장의 주어 자리에는 whether만 가능하고 if는 불가능하지만, 진주어 자리라면 둘 다 가능하다.

127 Whether she will come doesn't matter.

128 Whether it rains or not is a serious problem to delivery men.

129 Whether the criminal who escaped from jail committed other crimes is not known.

130 It depends on you whether we take a taxi or not.

131 Real friends don't care whether you have the latest clothes or a new phone.

132 I don't know if he will come to the party or not.

133 She asked me if Jake attended the meeting.

127 Whether she will come doesn't matter.

  [해석] 그녀가 올지 안 올지는 중요하지 않다.
  KILLER
  [whether S + V] 주어 (if 불가)

128 Whether it rains or not is a serious problem to delivery men.

  [해석] 비가 오는지 안 오는지는 배달부에게는 심각한 문제이다.
  KILLER
  [whether S + V] 주어 (if 불가)

129 Whether the criminal who escaped from jail committed other crimes is not known.

  [해석] 탈옥한 범인이 다른 범죄를 저질렀는지는 알려지지 않았다.
  KILLER
  [whether S + V] 주어 (if 불가)

  VOCA
  commit 저지르다

130 It depends on you whether we take a taxi or not.

  [해석] 우리가 택시를 타느냐 안 타느냐는 너에게 달려 있다.
  KILLER
  [whether S + V] 진주어 (if 가능)

131 Real friends don't care whether you have the latest clothes or a new phone.

  [해석] 진짜 친구는 네가 최신의 옷이나 새 폰을 갖고 있는지에 신경 쓰지 않는다.
  KILLER
  [whether S + V] 목적어 (if 가능)

132 I don't know if he will come to the party or not.

  [해석] 나는 그가 파티에 올지 안 올지 모른다.
  KILLER
  [if S + V] 목적어 (whether 가능)

133 She asked me if Jake attended the meeting.

  [해석] 그녀는 나에게 Jake가 회의에 참석했는지를 물었다.
  KILLER
  [if S + V] 목적어 (whether 불가)

134 The question is whether I should go abroad or stay here.

135 I'm wondering whether you would be willing to be a guest on one of our programs.

136 What is at issue is whether she was responsible for her actions.

137 I caught a cold and asked whether Helen could take over for me.

138 I have doubts about whether what she said is true.

139 The biggest problem with managing computer programmers is that you can never tell whether they are working by just looking at them.

134 The question is whether I should go abroad or stay here.

해석 : 문제는 내가 해외로 갈 것인가 아니면 여기에 머물 것인가 하는 것이다.
KILLER :
[whether S + V] 보어 (if 불가)

135 I'm wondering whether you would be willing to be a guest on one of our programs.

해석 : 당신이 우리의 프로그램 중 하나에 기꺼이 출연해 주실 수 있을지 궁금합니다.
KILLER :
- [whether S + V] 목적어 (if 가능)
- be willing to V : 기꺼이 ~하다
- one of 복수명사 (+ 단수동사) : ~ 중 하나

VOCA
willing 기꺼이 하는, 자발적인, 적극적인
(↔ unwilling, reluctant 꺼리는)

136 What is at issue is whether she was responsible for her actions.

해석 : 쟁점이 되고 있는 것은 그녀가 자기 행동에 대해 책임을 졌는지의 여부이다.
KILLER :
[whether S + V] 보어 (if 불가)

VOCA
be at issue 문제이다
be responsible for ~에 책임을 지다

137 I caught a cold and asked whether Helen could take over for me.

해석 : 나는 감기에 걸려서 Helen이 나를 대신할 수 있는지 물었다.
KILLER :
[whether S + V] 목적어 (if 가능)

VOCA
catch a cold 감기에 걸리다
take over (1) (임무를) 떠맡다, (사업을) 인수하다
(2) 점령하다, 장악하다
(3) 대신하다

138 I have doubts about whether what she said is true.

해석 : 그녀의 말이 사실인지 의심스럽다.
KILLER :
[whether S + V] 전치사의 목적어 (if 불가)

139 The biggest problem with managing computer programmers is that you can never tell whether they are working by just looking at them.

해석 : 컴퓨터 프로그래머를 관리하는 데 있어 가장 큰 문제는 단순히 바라보는 것을 통해서는 그들이 일하고 있는지 절대 알 수 없다는 것이다.
KILLER :
- [whether S + V] 전치사의 목적어 (if 불가)
- by Ving : ~함으로써, ~하는 것을 통해

VOCA
manage 관리하다
tell (1) 말하다 (2) 알다, 판단하다

140 The question arises as to whether the architect was aware of the situation.

141 The interview is the deciding factor in whether you will be hired or not.

142 The rent is the same irrespective of whether there are three or four occupants.

143 The test of a great book is whether we want to read it only once or more than once.

144 The main topic of discussion was whether or not there ought to be limits on artificial intelligence research.

145 It has not been proven whether the rumors spread in the X-files are true or not, but many believe them anyway.

140 The question arises as to whether the architect was aware of the situation.

[해석] 건축가가 그 상황에 대해 알고 있었느냐 아니냐는 의문이 생긴다.
KILLER
- [whether S + V] 전치사의 목적어 (if 불가)
- as to ~ situation은 the question을 수식하는 전치사 덩어리이다.

VOCA
arise 생기다, 발생하다
as to (전치사) ~에 대하여
(= about, regarding)
architect 건축가
be aware of ~를 알다, 인지하다

141 The interview is the deciding factor in whether you will be hired or not.

[해석] 그 면접이 네가 채용될지 말지를 결정하는 결정적인 요소이다.
KILLER
[whether S + V] 전치사의 목적어 (if 불가)

VOCA
deciding 결정적인
(= decisive, crucial, definite, conclusive)
factor 요소

142 The rent is the same irrespective of whether there are three or four occupants.

[해석] 거주자가 세 명이든 네 명이든 관계없이 집세는 동일하다.
KILLER
[whether S + V] 전치사의 목적어 (if 불가)

VOCA
irrespective of (전치사) ~에 상관없이
(= regardless of)
occupant 사용자, 입주자, 거주자

143 The test of a great book is whether we want to read it only once or more than once.

[해석] 훌륭한 책의 기준은 우리가 그것을 단지 한 번 또는 한 번 이상 읽기 원하는지 아닌지이다.
KILLER
[whether S + V] 보어 (if 불가)

VOCA
test 기준, 척도

144 The main topic of discussion was whether or not there ought to be limits on artificial intelligence research.

[해석] 이번 토론의 주요 논점은 인공지능 연구에 제한이 있어야 할지 말지였다.
KILLER
[whether S + V] 보어 (if 불가)

145 It has not been proven whether the rumors spread in the X-files are true or not, but many believe them anyway.

[해석] X 파일속에 펼쳐진 루머가 진짜인지 아닌지는 증명되지 않았지만, 어쨌든 많은 사람들이 그것을 믿고 있다.
KILLER
[whether S + V] 진주어 (if 가능)

VOCA
prove (1) ~인 것으로 드러나다
(2) 증명하다
spread 펼치다
(spread-spread-spread)
anyway 어쨌든

146 When I asked you whether the plaintiff had grabbed the knife, at first you answered that he could not have reached it, and the second time you said that he must have grabbed it.

> **(6) 간접 의문문 (의문사 S + V)**
> - 간접 의문문은 명사 취급을 받는다.
> - 간접 의문문은 주어, 목적어, 보어 자리에 쓰일 수 있다.
> - '의문사 to V'의 형태로 축약하여 쓸 수 있다.
>
> ① when S + V (언제 S가 V했는지) → when to V (언제 V했는지)
> ② where S + V (어디에서 S가 V했는지) → where to V (어디에서 V했는지)
> ③ why S + V (왜 S가 V했는지)
> ④ how S + V (어떻게 S가 V했는지) → how to V (어떻게 V했는지)
>   how 형/부 S + V (얼마나 형/부하게 S가 V할지)

147 When he arrived is not certain.

148 I don't know when he will come tomorrow.

149 I asked my son where he was hiding.

150 Sandy tried to explain why she was late.

151 This is why the leaves lose their green color.

146 When I asked you whether the plaintiff had grabbed the knife, at first you answered that he could not have reached it, and the second time you said that he must have grabbed it.

해석 내가 당신에게 원고가 칼을 잡았는지 물었을 때, 처음에 당신은 그의 손이 닿았을 리가 없다고 대답했는데, 두 번째는 확실히 잡았음에 틀림없다고 말했다.
KILLER
- [whether S + V] 목적어 (if 가능)
- could(= can) not have p.p : ~했을 리가 없다
- must have p.p : ~했음이 분명하다

VOCA
plaintiff 원고, 고소인
(↔ defendant 피고)
grab 쥐다, 잡다
reach (1) 도착하다
       (2) (손을 뻗어) 잡다

147 When he arrived is not certain.

해석 언제 그가 도착했는지는 확실하지 않다.
KILLER
[when S + V] 주어

148 I don't know when he will come tomorrow.

해석 나는 내일 언제 그가 도착할지 모른다.
KILLER
- [when S + V] 목적어
- 이 문장에서 [when S + V]은 종속절(= 부사절)이 아니므로, 시조부현미의 영향을 받지 않기 때문에 필요하다면 will을 쓸 수 있다.

149 I asked my son where he was hiding.

해석 나는 아들에게 어디에 그가 숨어있었는지를 물어보았다.
KILLER
[where S + V] 목적어

150 Sandy tried to explain why she was late.

해석 Sandy는 왜 그녀가 늦었는지를 설명하려고 노력했다.
KILLER
[why S + V] 목적어

151 This is why the leaves lose their green color.

해석 그래서 잎들이 초록색을 잃는 것이다.
KILLER
[why S + V] 보어

152 Officers could not reveal how he died.

153 They were amazed at how accurate the test was.

154 I wanted to show off how well I spoke French.

155 We evaluated how effectively the policy was working.

156 The mystery is how he solved the problem.

157 I wonder how fast he solved the problem.

158 Botanists are not sure where the first plant on earth was grown or even what plant it was.

152 Officers could not reveal how he died.

[해석] 경찰관들은 어떻게 그가 죽었는지 밝혀낼 수 없었다.
KILLER
[how S + V] 목적어

VOCA
officer 경찰관
official 공무원
reveal 밝혀내다

153 They were amazed at how accurate the test was.

[해석] 그들은 얼마나 그 테스트가 정확한지를 보고 깜짝 놀랐다.
KILLER
[how 형/부 S + V] 전치사의 목적어

VOCA
accurate 정확한(= precise)

154 I wanted to show off how well I spoke French.

[해석] 나는 내가 프랑스어를 얼마나 잘하는지 자랑하고 싶었다.
KILLER
[how 형/부 S + V] 목적어

VOCA
show off 자랑하다
well (부사) 잘

155 We evaluated how effectively the policy was working.

[해석] 우리는 그 정책이 얼마나 효율적으로 작용하고 있었는지 평가했다.
KILLER
• [how 형/부 S + V] 목적어
• effectively는 동사 was working을 수식한다.

VOCA
evaluate 평가하다
(= appraise, assess)
work 작동하다, 작용하다

156 The mystery is how he solved the problem.

[해석] 수수께끼는 그가 그 문제를 어떻게 해결했는가 하는 것이다.
KILLER
[how S + V] 보어

157 I wonder how fast he solved the problem.

[해석] 그가 그 문제를 얼마나 빨리 해결했는지 궁금하다.
KILLER
[how 형/부 S + V] 목적어

158 Botanists are not sure where the first plant on earth was grown or even what plant it was.

[해석] 식물학자들은 지구상의 첫 번째 식물이 어디서 자랐는지, 심지어 어떤 식물이었는지도 확신하지 못한다.
KILLER
[where S + V] 목적어

VOCA
botanist 식물학자

159 I am going to explain why these actions are being taken and what they mean for our company.

160 Wandering tribesmen had to know how they could cross deserts safely without dying of thirst.

161 Why people start talking about the weather or current events is that they are harmless and common to everyone.

162 If you've got ambition, you can rise to the top of your chosen profession regardless of when and where you started out.

163 The question of how powerful a media organization is is difficult to cope with.

159 I am going to explain why these actions are being taken and what they mean for our company.

　해석 저는 왜 이러한 조치가 취해졌는지와 그것이 우리 회사에 어떤 의미를 갖는지 설명 드리고자 합니다.
　KILLER
- [why S+V]와 [what 불] 목적어
- are being taken : 진행시제, 수동태

VOCA
action 조치(= measure)

160 Wandering tribesmen had to know how they could cross deserts safely without dying of thirst.

　해석 이리저리 돌아다니며 사는 부족민들은 갈증으로 죽지 않고 안전하게 사막을 건널 수 있는 방법을 알 필요가 있다.
　KILLER
- [how S+V] 목적어
- without Ving : ~하지 않고

VOCA
tribesman 부족민
die of ~로 죽다

161 Why people start talking about the weather or current events is that they are harmless and common to everyone.

　해석 날씨나 최근 사건들에 대해서 사람들이 이야기를 시작하는 이유는 그것들이 모두에게 아무런 해가 없는 공통되는 소재이기 때문이다.
　KILLER
- [why S+V] 주어
- talk는 자동사이므로 전치사 about이 필요하다.

VOCA
current event 최근의 사건
harmless 무해한(= innocuous)

162 If you've got ambition, you can rise to the top of your chosen profession regardless of when and where you started out.

　해석 만약 당신이 야망을 가지고 있다면, 당신이 언제 어디서 시작했는지에 상관없이 여러분이 선택한 직업의 정상에 오를 수 있습니다.
　KILLER
- [when and where S+V] 전치사의 목적어
- rise는 자동사이므로 이하의 전치사와 어울린다.
- 과거분사 chosen은 명사 profession을 수식한다.

VOCA
ambition 야망
profession 직업
regardless of (전) ~에 상관없이

163 The question of how powerful a media organization is is difficult to cope with.

　해석 한 언론 조직이 얼마나 강력한가의 질문은 대처하기가 어렵다
　KILLER
- [how 형부 S+V] 전치사의 목적어
- 부정사(to cope with)의 목적어가 문장의 주어(the question)와 같아서 삭제되었다.

164 Not many patients in whom cancer develops to this stage survive, which is why it is so important to treat cancer early.

> **(7) 의문사 to V**
>
> ① when to V (언제 V했는지)
> ② where to V (어디에서 V했는지)
> ③ how to V (어떻게 V했는지)
> ④ what to V (무엇을 V할지)

165 She doesn't know when to stop talking.

166 I know where to draw the line.

167 What to do next is not decided yet.

168 How to solve the problems is the question.

169 The problem is not when to go but how to go there.

164 Not many patients in whom cancer develops to this stage survive, which is why it is so important to treat cancer early.

해석 암이 이 단계까지 진행되는 환자의 대다수가 살아남지 못하는데, 그래서 암을 조기에 치료하는 것이 매우 중요하다.
KILLER
- [why S+V] 보어
- 전치사 whom 뒤에는 완벽한 문장이 쓰인다.
- '발병하다'라고 해석되는 develop는 자동사이다.
- early는 형용사이기도 하고 부사이기도 하다.

VOCA
patient 환자
develop 성장하다, 발달하다, 개발하다, (병이) 생기다, 진행하다
treat 대접하다, 처리하다

165 She doesn't know when to stop talking.

해석 그녀는 언제 입을 다물어야 할지를 모른다.
KILLER
[when to V] 목적어

166 I know where to draw the line.

해석 나는 어디에 선을 그어야 할지를 안다.
KILLER
[where S+V] 목적어

167 What to do next is not decided yet.

해석 다음에 무엇을 할지는 아직 정해지지 않았다.
KILLER
[what to V] 주어

168 How to solve the problems is the question.

해석 어떻게 문제를 해결할지가 질문이다.
KILLER
[how to V] 주어

169 The problem is not when to go but how to go there.

해석 문제는 언제 갈 것인지가 아니라 어떻게 그곳에 갈 것인지이다.
KILLER
- [when to V], [how to V] 보어
- not A but B: A가 아니라 B

170 Education ought to teach not just how to make a living, but how to live a life.

171 Instead of spending time trying to suppress emotions, it is better to learn how to manage them well.

172 Have you made up your mind about where to put all these things?

173 They deliberated on whether to continue with the talks.

174 There is always controversy as to when to put up a christmas tree and when to take it down.

175 One should be able to distinguish between what to do and what not to do.

170 Education ought to teach not just how to make a living, but how to live a life.

> 해석: 교육은 어떻게 생계를 꾸려나갈까 뿐만 아니라 어떻게 인생을 살아나갈까를 가르쳐야

KILLER
- [how to V] 목적어
- not just A but B = not only A but also B : A뿐만 아니라 B도

VOCA
make a living 생계를 꾸리다

171 Instead of spending time trying to suppress emotions, it is better to learn how to manage them well.

> 해석: 감정을 억제하는 데 시간을 보내는 대신, 감정을 잘 관리하는 방법을 배우는 것이 더 낫다.

KILLER
- [how to V] 목적어
- instead of(~대신에)는 전치사이므로 명사 또는 동명사를 목적어로 취한다.
- spend 시간/돈/노력 (in) Ving : Ving하는 데에 시간/돈/노력을 쓰다
- 복수대명사 them은 emotions를 가리키므로 단수 it으로 쓸 수 없다.
- 부사 well은 동사 manage를 수식한다. 형용사 good은 불가능하다.

VOCA
suppress 억제하다

172 Have you made up your mind about where to put all these things?

> 해석: 이 모든 것들을 어디에 두어야 할지 결정하셨나요?

KILLER
[where to V] 목적어

VOCA
make up one's mind 결심하다

173 They deliberated on whether to continue with the talks.

> 해석: 그들은 그 회담을 계속할 것인지를 고민했다.

KILLER
[whether to V (V를 할지 말지)] 전치사의 목적어

VOCA
deliberate on 신중히 생각하다, 숙고하다

174 There is always controversy as to when to put up a christmas tree and when to take it down.

> 해석: 크리스마스 트리를 언제 준비할 것이며 또 언제 치울 것인가에 대한 논쟁은 언제나 있다.

KILLER
- [when to V] 전치사의 목적어
- 이어동사(take down)의 목적어가 대명사일 경우, 동사와 부사 사이에 위치해야 한다.

VOCA
controversy 논쟁
as to (전) ~에 대해(= about)
take down 분해하다, 치우다

175 One should be able to distinguish between what to do and what not to do.

> 해석: 해야 할 일과 하지 말아야 할 일을 분별할 줄 알아야 한다.

KILLER
- [what to V] 전치사의 목적어
- 부정사(to do)를 부정사는 not은 앞에 배치하는 것이 원칙이다.

176 No one can tell you what school to choose.

177 One of the puzzles still bewildering biologists is how cells know what to become in an embryo.

178 The problem lies in how to allocate the expenses and how to prepare the money required.

내 인생 **마지막 기본 영어구문**

176 No one can tell you what school to choose.

해석 아무도 너에게 어떤 학교를 선택할지를 말할 수 없다.
KILLER
[what N to V (어떤 N를 V해야할지)] 목적어

177 One of the puzzles still bewildering biologists is how cells know what to become in an embryo.

해석 생물학자들을 여전히 어리둥절하게 만드는 퍼즐 중 하나는 세포가 태아에서 무엇이 되어야 하는지 어떻게 아는가이다.
KILLER
• [what to V] 목적어
• one of the 복수명사 (puzzles) + 단수동사 (is)
• 현재분사 bewildering biologists는 puzzles를 후치 수식한다.

VOCA
bewilder 어리둥절하게 하다, 혼란스럽게 만들다
(= perplex, confuse, baffle)
embryo 배아

178 The problem lies in how to allocate the expenses and how to prepare the money required.

해석 문제는 어떻게 비용을 배분하는가와 어떻게 필요한 예산을 마련하는가에 있다.
KILLER
• [how to V] 전치사의 목적어
• 과거분사 required는 money를 후치수식한다.

VOCA
lie in ~에 놓여있다
allocate 할당하다, 배분하다
expense 비용

 **김태은 영어**

마지막 기본 영어구문

CHAPTER

02

여러 가지 동사의 모습 파악하기

1. 자동사
2. 타동사
3. 시제 x 태

여러 가지 동사의 모습 파악하기

(1) 동사는 크게 자동사와 타동사로 나누어진다.

(2) 자동사는 주어의 존재나 상태를 나타내는 동사로, 이하에 목적어를 취할 수 없으며 수동태로 쓰일 수 없다는 특징을 갖는다.

구분			능동	수동 (불가)
1	단순	현재	wait(s)	is/am/are waited (×)
2		과거	waited	was/were waited (×)
3		미래	will wait	will be waited (×)
4	완료	현재	have/has waited	have/has been waited (×)
5		과거	had waited	had been waited (×)
6		미래	will have waited	will have been waited (×)
7	진행	현재	is/am/are waiting	is/am/are being waited (×)
8		과거	was/were waiting	was/were being waited (×)
9		미래	will be waiting	will be waited (×)
10	완료 진행	현재	have/has been waiting	
11		과거	had been waiting	
12		미래	will have been waiting	

(3) 타동사는 주어의 동작 나타내는 동사로, 이하에 목적어를 취한다면 능동태, 목적어를 취하지 않는다면 수동태로 쓰여야 한다.

구분			능동 (타동사+목적어 있음)	수동 (타동사+목적어 없음)
1	단순	현재	write a letter	is/am/are written
2		과거	wrote a letter	was/were written
3		미래	will write a letter	will be written
4	완료	현재	have/has written a letter	have/has been written
5		과거	had written a letter	had been written
6		미래	will have written a letter	will have been written
7	진행	현재	is/am/are writing a letter	is/am/are being written
8		과거	was/were writing a letter	was/were being written
9		미래	will be writing a letter	will be written
10	완료 진행	현재	have/has been writing a letter	
11		과거	had been writing a letter	
12		미래	will have been writing a letter	

(4) 4형식 동사는 뒤에 명사가 있어도 수동태로 쓰일 수 있다.
   ① give
   ② offer
   ③ tell
   ④ show
   ⑤ teach
   ⑥ ask

(5) 명사를 목적격 보어로 취하는 5형식 동사 뒤에 명사가 있어도 수동태로 쓰일 수 있다.
   ① name
   ② call
   ③ elect
   ④ appoint
   ⑤ make

1 자동사

> (1) be동사

001 The kittens are in the basket.

002 She is a student.

003 She is bright and courteous.

004 He was running down the street.

005 Some children were wrongly sent to an orphanage.

006 One of the ways to find the right item for you is to take all the information into account and to carefully examine the differences.

001　The kittens are in the basket.

해석 새끼 고양이들이 바구니 안에 있다.
KILLER
1형식 be동사

002　She is a student.

해석 그녀는 학생이다.
KILLER
2형식 be동사 + 명사보어

003　She is bright and courteous.

해석 그녀는 밝고 예의바르다.
KILLER
2형식 be동사 + 형용사보어

004　He was running down the street.

해석 그는 거리를 달려 내려오고 있었다.
KILLER
be Ving : 진행시제

005　Some children were wrongly sent to an orphanage.

해석 몇몇 아이들은 고아원으로 잘못 보내졌다.
KILLER
be p.p : 수동태

006　One of the ways to find the right item for you is to take all the information into account and to carefully examine the differences.

해석 당신에게 맞는 물건을 찾는 방법들 중 하나는 모든 정보를 고려하고 신중하게 차이점들을 검토하는 것이다.
KILLER
• 2형식 be동사 + [to V] 보어 : ~라는 것이다
• one of 복수명사(ways) + 단수동사(is)

VOCA
take A into account A를 고려하다
examine 조사/검토/검사/진찰하다

007 One of the facts the investigators discovered was that the ship was overloaded with cargo including steel bars.

008 The most prevalent mistake made by amateur photographers is that they are not physically close enough to their subjects.

009 The amount of exports to Japan has been on the decrease over the five years.

(2) 1형식

010 Real power belongs to the few.

011 A thread of light emerged from the keyhole.

012 The terror attack resulted in countless civilian casualties.

007 One of the facts the investigators discovered was that the ship was overloaded with cargo including steel bars.

[해석] 조사관들이 밝혀낸 사실들 중 하나는 그 배가 강철봉을 포함하는 화물이 과적되었다는 것이었다.

KILLER
- 2형식 be동사 + [that + 완] 보어 : ~라는 것이다
- one of 복수명사 (facts) + 단수동사 (was)

VOCA
be overloaded with ~로 과적되다
cargo 화물
including ~를 포함하는

008 The most prevalent mistake made by amateur photographers is that they are not physically close enough to their subjects.

[해석] 아마추어 사진가에 의해 저질러지는 가장 흔한 실수는 그들이 피사체에 물리적으로 충분히 가까이 가지 못한다는 것이다.

KILLER
- 2형식 be동사 + [that + 완] 보어 : ~라는 것이다
- 형/부 enough to V : V할 정도로 충분히 형/부하다

VOCA
prevalent 흔한, 널리 퍼진
physically 물리적으로, 신체적으로
subject 과목, 주제, 피실험자, 피사체, 백성

009 The amount of exports to Japan has been on the decrease over the five years.

[해석] 일본으로의 수출 양은 5년 동안 감소해 왔다.

KILLER
- 1형식 be동사
- over the five years(5년에 걸쳐)는 선표현이므로 완료시제가 필요하다.

VOCA
be on the rise 증가하다
be on the decrease 감소하다

010 Real power belongs to the few.

[해석] 진정한 권력은 몇 명의 소수가 잡고 있다.

KILLER
1형식 자동사 belong (to)

011 A thread of light emerged from the keyhole.

[해석] 열쇠 구멍에서 한 줄기 불빛이 새어나오고 있었다.

KILLER
1형식 자동사 emerge

012 The terror attack resulted in countless civilian casualties.

[해석] 테러 공격으로 수많은 민간인 희생자들이 발생했다.

KILLER
1형식 자동사 result in + 결과 (~를 낳다)

VOCA
countless 수많은
civilian 민간인
casualty 사상자, 피해자

013 The evacuation of thousands of people in the city took place because of the earthquake.

014 The stately march that hundreds of soldiers participated in was very impressive.

015 He grew up with numbers and electronics and built his own computer at a young age.

016 Scientists suspect that genes allowing us to metabolize alcohol arose some 10 million years ago.

017 Despite the school's withdrawal of the plan, what began as a protest soon evolved into a bigger movement to criticize the university's unilateral and money-focused way.

013　The evacuation of thousands of people in the city took place because of the earthquake.

[해석] 지진으로 인해 그 도시에서 수천 명의 대피가 일어났다.

[KILLER]
- 1형식 자동사 took place
- 전치사 because of(= due to, owing to, on account of) vs. 접속사 because

VOCA
evacuation 대피, 철수, 피난
took place 발생하다, 실시되다

014　The stately march that hundreds of soldiers participated in was very impressive.

[해석] 수백 명의 군인들이 참여했던 위풍당당한 행군은 아주 인상적이었다.

[KILLER]
- 1형식 자동사 participate
- 목적격 관계대명사 that(생략 가능) + 전치사(in)의 목적어가 빠진 불완전한 문장 → in 필수

VOCA
stately 위풍당당한, 장중한, 위엄 있는
march 3월, 행군, 행진
impressive 인상적인

015　He grew up with numbers and electronics and built his own computer at a young age.

[해석] 그는 숫자와 전자기기를 다루며 자랐으며 어린 나이에 스스로 컴퓨터를 제작할 수 있었다.

[KILLER]
자동사 grow up(성장하다) vs. 타동사 bring up(양육하다, 키우다 = raise)

016　Scientists suspect that genes allowing us to metabolize alcohol arose some 10 million years ago.

[해석] 과학자들은 우리가 알코올을 소화하도록 허용하는 유전자가 대략 천만 년 전에 발생했다고 의심한다.

[KILLER]
- 1형식 자동사 arise – arose – arisen(생기다, 발생하다 = occur)
- suspect that S + V : ~라고 의심하다(that절 내부 주어는 genes, 동사는 arose)
- allow A to V : A가 V하도록 허락하다
- 접표현인 ~ago가 있으므로 arise는 과거시제로 쓰여야 한다.
- 숫자 앞의 some, about, around는 부사이고, '대략'이라고 해석한다.

VOCA
metabolize 신진대사시키다, 분해하여 소화하다

017　Despite the school's withdrawal of the plan, what began as a protest soon evolved into a bigger movement to criticize the university's unilateral and money-focused way.

[해석] 학교 측의 그 계획의 철수에도 불구하고, 항의로써 시작했던 것이 그 학교의 일방적이고 돈 위주의 방식을 비판하는 더 큰 움직임으로 곧 발달했다.

[KILLER]
- 1형식 자동사 evolve(발달하다, 진화하다) : evolve는 문맥에 따라 타동사(발달/전개시키다)도 가능하다.
- 전치사 despite(~에도 불구하고 = in spite of) vs. 접속사 although

VOCA
withdrawal 철회, 취소, 철수
unilateral 일방적인
N-focused (명사) 위주의

(3) 2형식

018 He became increasingly sedentary in later life.

019 Sport became the perfect outlet for his aggression.

020

    020-1 Animals remain alert all the time.

    020-2 Animals subject to unpredictable attacks remain alert all the time.

021 The gift of time gets more satisfying and more valuable than money.

022 She looked tired and lonely, and her eyes were fixed firmly on the ground.

내 인생 마지막 기본 영어구문

018 He <u>became</u> increasingly sedentary in later life.

[해석] 그는 노년기에 점점 더 앉아서 지내게 되었다.
[KILLER]
2형식 자동사 become + 형용사 보어 sedentary

[VOCA]
sedentary 앉아서 지내는, 앉아서 하는

019 Sport <u>became</u> the perfect outlet for his aggression.

[해석] 스포츠는 그의 공격성에 대한 완벽한 배출구였다.
[KILLER]
2형식 자동사 become + 명사 보어 the perfect outlet

[VOCA]
outlet 배출구
aggression 공격성

020

020-1 Animals <u>remain</u> alert all the time.

[해석] 동물들은 항상 경계심을 유지한다.
[KILLER]
2형식 remain + 형용사 보어 alert

[VOCA]
alert 정신이 깨어있는, 경계하는, 방심하지 않는(= vigilant)

020-2 Animals subject to unpredictable attacks <u>remain</u> alert all the time.

[해석] 예측할 수 없는 공격의 대상인 동물은 항상 경계 태세를 유지한다.
[KILLER]
(subject to ~ attacks)는 animals를 후치 수식하는 형용사 덩어리

[VOCA]
be subject to ~의 대상이다, ~를 받다

021 The gift of time <u>gets</u> more satisfying and more valuable than money.

[해석] 시간이라는 선물은 돈보다 더 만족스럽고 가치 있어진다.
[KILLER]
• 2형식 get + 형용사 보어 satisfying and valuable
• gift of time을 수식하는 감정분사 satisfying

022 She <u>looked</u> tired and lonely, and her eyes were fixed firmly on the ground.

[해석] 그녀는 피곤하고 외로워 보였고, 눈은 땅바닥에 단단히 고정되어 있었다.
[KILLER]
• 2형식 look + 형용사 보어 tired and lonely
• she를 수식하는 감정분사 tired

[VOCA]
be fixed on ~에 고정되다
firmly 단단히

023 She ran home after she grew frustrated with the negative attitudes her friends displayed.

024 Chances of an asteroid actually hitting Earth seem very unlikely, but scientists keep an eye on it.

내 인생 마지막 기본 영어구문

023　She ran home after she <u>grew</u> frustrated with the negative attitudes her friends displayed.

해석 그녀는 친구들이 보인 부정적인 태도에 좌절감을 느낀 후 집으로 달려갔다.

KILLER
- 2형식 grow + 형용사 보어 frustrated
- attitudes 뒤에 목적격 관계대명사가 생략되어 있다.
- 동사 뒤에서 home은 종종 부사로 쓰이며, '집에, 집으로'라고 해석된다. → go to home (X)

VOCA
display 내보이다, 전시하다

024　Chances of an asteroid actually hitting Earth <u>seem</u> very unlikely, but scientists keep an eye on it.

해석 실제로 지구에 충돌할 가능성은 매우 가능성이 낮게 느껴지지만, 과학자들은 소행성을 주시하고 있다.

KILLER
2형식 grow + 형용사 보어 frustrated

VOCA
chances 가능성, 확률
unlikely (형) 가능성이 낮은
keep an eye on ~를 지켜보다, 감시하다
asteroid 소행성

Chapter 02 여러 가지 동사의 모습 파악하기

2 타동사

(1) 3형식 동사와 여러 가지 목적어

〈3형식 동사 + 명사 목적어〉

025 The desk hampered people's movement.

026 A good teacher encourages creative and critical thinking.

027 The government took measures to promote domestic industry.

028 25% of the prescription contains substances which are derived from wild plants.

029 Emotional eaters manipulate their own mental conditions and manifest their problems in lots of incomprehensible ways.

030 The international community has eventually reached a point of zero tolerance toward North Korea's endless game of carrot and stick and other provocations.

025 The desk hampered people's movement.

해석 그 책상이 사람들의 움직임을 방해했다.

KILLER
타동사 hamper(방해하다) + 명사 목적어

VOCA
hamper 방해하다(= impede, hinder)

---

026 A good teacher encourages creative and critical thinking.

해석 좋은 교사는 창의적이고 비판적인 사고를 장려한다.

KILLER
타동사 encourage(격려/장려하다) + 명사 목적어

VOCA
critical thinking 비판적 사고

---

027 The government took measures to promote domestic industry.

해석 정부는 국내 산업을 증진시킬 조치를 취했다.

KILLER
- 타동사 take(취하다) + measures(조치)
- (to promote domestic industry)는 measures를 후치수식하는 부정사의 형용사적 용법이다.

VOCA
take measures 조치를 취하다

---

028 25% of the prescription contains substances which are derived from wild plants.

해석 그 처방전의 25%는 야생 식물에서부터 나온 물질들을 포함한다.

KILLER
- 타동사 contain(포함하다) + 명사 목적어
- 주어가 '부분(%) of 명사' 구조이므로 뒤에 있는 명사(prescription)가 동사의 수를 결정한다.
- 주격 관계대명사 which 뒤의 동사의 수(are)는 선행사(substances)에 일치된다.

VOCA
prescription 처방전
substance 물질
be derived from ~로부터 나오다

---

029 Emotional eaters manipulate their own mental conditions and manifest their problems in lots of incomprehensible ways.

해석 감정적으로 먹는 사람들은 스스로의 정신 상태를 조종하며 많은 이해하기 힘든 방식으로 그들의 문제를 나타낸다.

KILLER
- 타동사 manipulate(조종하다) + 명사 목적어
- 타동사 manifest(보여준다) + 명사 목적어

VOCA
manipulate 조작하다, 조종하다
manifest 나타내다, 보여주다
incomprehensible 이해할 수 없는
in ~ ways ~한 방식으로

---

030 The international community has eventually reached a point of zero tolerance toward North Korea's endless game of carrot and stick and other provocations.

해석 국제 사회는 북한의 끊임없는 당근과 채찍 게임과 다른 도발 행위에 대해 결국 무관용 정책에 도달했다.

KILLER
- 타동사 reach(도달하다) + 명사 목적어
- another + 단수명사 vs. other + 복수명사

VOCA
tolerance 관용
zero tolerance 무관용, 엄중 처벌 원칙
carrot and stick 당근과 채찍, 회유와 협박
provocation 도발, 자극

⟨3형식 동사 + 부정사 목적어⟩

031 The company has planned to enter the digital TV chip market.

032 The riot police quickly sought to distance themselves from the protesters.

033 She is such a meddlesome person and wants to tell everybody in town what to do.

034 When mountaineers attempt to climb high peaks, they avoid altitude sickness by climbing to one level and then resting for a few days.

035 He managed to conquer his sickness, but succumbed to intense pain in his shoulder.

내 인생 **마지막 기본 영어구문**

031 The company has planned to enter the digital TV chip market.

> 해석 그 회사는 디지털 TV 칩 시장에 진입할 계획이다.
> KILLER
> • 3형식 plan + to V: ~할 계획을 세우다
> • enter 들어가다 vs. enter into 시작하다

032 The riot police quickly sought to distance themselves from the protesters.

> 해석 전투 경찰은 재빨리 시위자들에게서 멀어지려고 노력했다.
> KILLER
> • 3형식 seek + to V: ~하려고 노력하다, 시도하다
> • 주어와 목적어가 같다면, 목적어 자리에 재귀대명사(themselves)를 써야 한다.
> • the police는 복수 취급이므로 재귀대명사를 단수형 himself가 아니라 복수형으로 쓴다.
> • distance는 동사로 쓰인다면 '떨어트리다, 거리를 두다'라고 해석된다.

VOCA
distance A from B
A를 B로부터 떨어트리다

033 She is such a meddlesome person and wants to tell everybody in town what to do.

> 해석 그녀는 매우 참견하기 좋아하는 사람이고, 마을의 모든 사람들에게 이래라 저래라 말하고 싶어 한다.
> KILLER
> • 3형식 want + to V: ~하고자 하다, ~하길 원하다
> • such a 형 명 = so 형 a 명: 매우 (형용사)한 (명사)
> • what to V: 무엇을 V해야 할지
> 참고
> She is **such** a meddlesome person **that** she wants to tell everybody in town what to do.

VOCA
meddlesome 참견하기 좋아하는

034 When mountaineers attempt to climb high peaks, they avoid altitude sickness by climbing to one level and then resting for a few days.

> 해석 산악인들이 높은 봉우리에 오르려고 시도할 때, 그들은 한 단계까지 오른 다음 며칠 동안 쉬는 것으로 고산병을 피한다.
> KILLER
> • 3형식 attempt + to V: ~하려고 시도하다
> • be Ving: ~함으로써 (climbing, resting으로 동명사 병치)

VOCA
altitude sickness 고산병

035 He managed to conquer his sickness, but succumbed to intense pain in his shoulder.

> 해석 그는 병을 극복하는 데 성공했지만, 어깨의 심한 통증에는 굴복했다.
> KILLER
> 3형식 manage + to V: 가까스로/간신히 ~하다

VOCA
conquer 정복하다, 이겨내다
succumb (to) (자) 굴복하다, 항복하다
(= submit, yield, surrender, give in)

Chapter 02 여러 가지 동사의 모습 파악하기

⟨3형식 동사 + 동명사 목적어⟩

036 His brother enjoyed pointing out the errors in his essays.

037 Clients appreciated having all the services in one place and being given very practical advice on diet.

038 Those who had resisted eating the marshmallow had better school grades and social success than those who ate the marshmallow straight away.

039 Instead of insisting on finding the best possible decision, we are determined to accept one that seems good enough.

내 인생 **마지막 기본 영어구문**

036 His brother enjoyed pointing out the errors in his essays.

:해석: 그의 형은 그가 쓴 에세이의 오류를 지적하는 것을 즐겼다.
:KILLER:
3형식 enjoy + Ving : ~를 즐기다, 누리다

VOCA
point out ⑴ 가리키다 ⑵ 지적하다

037 Clients appreciated having all the services in one place and being given very practical advice on diet.

:해석: 고객들은 모든 서비스를 한 곳에서 받고 식단에 대한 매우 실용적인 조언을 받는 것을 고마워했다.
:KILLER:
- appreciate + Ving : ~를 감사하다
- appreciate는 사람을 목적어로 취할 수 없다. (I appreciate you.(X) → Thank you.)
- be given + N : (명사)를 받다

VOCA
practical 실용적인(= pragmatic)

038 Those who had resisted eating the marshmallow had better school grades and social success than those who ate the marshmallow straight away.

:해석: 마시멜로 먹는 것을 참고 견딘 사람들이 곧바로 마시멜로를 먹어 버린 사람들보다 성적도 더 좋고 사회적으로도 더 성공했다.
:KILLER:
- resist + Ving : ⑴ ~에 저항하다, 견디다 ⑵ 반대하다
- 비교급 better이 있으므로 than(~보다)을 통해 비교 대상을 표시할 수 있다.
- those who : ~한 사람들

039 Instead of insisting on finding the best possible decision, we are determined to accept one that seems good enough.

:해석: 가능한 한 최선의 결정을 찾는 것을 고집하는 대신, 우리는 종종 충분히 좋게 보이는 결정을 받아들이기로 결심했다.
:KILLER:
- 전치사 instead of(~대신에) + 명사 또는 Ving
- insist on + 명사 또는 Ving : ~를 고집하다
- be determined to V : ~하겠다고 결심하다(= decide, resolve)
- enough가 부사로 쓰일 때에는 반드시 후치수식해야 한다. (enough good : X)

⟨3형식 동사 + 부정사/동명사 목적어 구분⟩

040 We stopped to take a break.

041 We stopped taking a break.

042 I've never for a moment regretted marrying you.

043 We regret to inform you that your application has not been successful.

044 When I arrived at the restaurant, I apologized and told my wife that I didn't mean to be late.

045 Emotional leadership means understanding your impact on others and then adjusting your style accordingly.

040 We stopped to take a break.

해석 우리는 쉬기 위해 멈추었다.
KILLER
stop to V : ~하기 위해 멈추다

041 We stopped taking a break.

해석 우리는 쉬는 것을 멈추었다.
KILLER
stop Ving : ~하는 것을 멈추다

042 I've never for a moment regretted marrying you.

해석 나는 한 순간도 너와 결혼한 것을 후회한 적이 없다.
KILLER
- regret Ving : ~했던 것을 후회하다
- have never p.p : ~해본 적 없다
- for a moment 잠깐 동안

043 We regret to inform you that your application has not been successful.

해석 귀하의 지원이 성공적이지 못했음을 알려드리게 되어 유감입니다.
KILLER
- regret to V : ~하게 되어 유감이다 vs. regret Ving : ~했던 것을 후회하다
- inform 사람 that S+V : (사람)에게 S+V를 알려주다, 고지하다

044 When I arrived at the restaurant, I apologized and told my wife that I didn't mean to be late.

해석 식당에 도착했을 때, 나는 사과했고 아내에게 늦을 의도는 없었다고 말했다.
KILLER
- mean to V : ~할 의도이다, 작정이다
- arrive와 apologize는 자동사이다.

045 Emotional leadership means understanding your impact on others and then adjusting your style accordingly.

해석 감정적 리더십은 다른 사람에게 미치는 영향을 이해하고 그에 따라 스타일을 조정하는 것을 의미한다.
KILLER
mean Ving : ~를 의미하다, 뜻하다 (동명사 목적어 and 병치)

VOCA
adjust 조정하다, 조절하다, 적응하다
accordingly 그에 따라, 그에 맞추어

046 The turtle stopped breathing air through his nose and mouth long ago. Instead, it takes in air through its skin and an opening under its tail.

047 This government pushing a cigarette price increase means to discourage people from smoking and give the state more revenue from taxes imposed on each pack.

⟨3형식 동사 + that/what 목적어⟩

048 They claim that they have nothing to hide.

049 I suggested that she try the local library.

050 For a long time, people did not know that the heart pumps blood in the body.

051 He was there and saw what happened, so his seems like the only authentic account.

046 The turtle stopped breathing air through his nose and mouth long ago. Instead, it takes in air through its skin and an opening under its tail.

[해석] 거북이는 오래전에 코와 입을 통해 공기를 마시는 것을 멈추었다. 대신, 그것은 피부와 꼬리 아래의 구멍을 통해 공기를 들이마신다.

KILLER
stop Ving : ~하는 것을 멈추다

VOCA
instead, 그 대신에
opening (1) 구멍, 틈 (2) 시작
take in (1) 섭취하다
         (2) 받아들이다
         (3) 속이다(= deceive)
         (4) (집에) 들이다

047 This government pushing a cigarette price increase means to discourage people from smoking and give the state more revenue from taxes imposed on each pack.

[해석] 담배 가격 인상을 밀어붙이고 있는 이번 정부는 국가에게 한 갑마다 부과된 세금으로부터의 수입을 확보해 주면서, 사람들이 흡연하는 것을 막을 의도이다.

KILLER
• mean to V : ~할 작정이다, 의도이다
• pushing ~ price는 주어인 the government를 후치수식하는 현재분사이다.
• discourage A from Ving : A가 Ving하는 것을 막다
• 동사원형 discourage와 give가 병치되어 있다. (give, to give 둘 다 가능)
• imposed ~ pack은 taxes를 후치수식하는 과거분사이다.

VOCA
price increase 가격 인상
state (명사) (1) 상태 (2) 국가
       (동사) 진술하다, 말하다

048 They claim that they have nothing to hide.

[해석] 그들은 숨길 것이 아무것도 없다고 주장한다.

KILLER
claim [that + 완] : ~라고 주장하다

049 I suggested that she try the local library.

[해석] 나는 그녀가 지역 도서관을 찾아보아야 한다고 주장했다.

KILLER
suggest [that + 완] : ~해야 한다고 주장하다 (주요명제 → 동사원형 try)

050 For a long time, people did not know that the heart pumps blood in the body.

[해석] 오랫동안, 사람들은 몸속에서 심장이 혈액을 펌프질한다는 것을 알지 못했다.

KILLER
know [that + 완] : ~를 알다

051 He was there and saw what happened, so his seems like the only authentic account.

[해석] 그는 그 자리에 있었고 무슨 일이 일어났는지를 보았고, 그래서 그의 것이 유일하게 믿을 만한 설명이다.

KILLER
• see [what + 불]
• his는 소유격으로 다른 명사와 함께 쓰일 수도 있고, 소유대명사로 단독으로 쓰일 수도 있다.
• seem + 형용사(~하게 보인다) vs. seem like + 명사(~인 것처럼 보인다)

VOCA
the only 유일한
authentic 진실된, 진짜인(= genuine)

052 Researchers say that reality TV programs offer consumers several benefits including satisfying their curiosity.

053 In the near future, I believe that most people will wear user-friendly equipment making their daily lives even more convenient.

054 To say that we should try to be a better person does not necessarily mean that we have to curb our anger all the time.

055 This result moved that a policy maker be concerned with the cultural context.

056 Asked to recall what they had seen, they remembered only negative things about the incident.

내 인생 마지막 기본 영어구문

052 Researchers <u>say that reality TV programs offer consumers several benefits including satisfying their curiosity.</u>

> **해석** 연구원들은 리얼리티 TV 프로그램이 그들의 호기심을 만족시키는 것을 포함하여 소비자들에게 몇 가지 이점을 제공한다고 말한다.

KILLER
- say [that + 완] : ~라고 말하다
- (including ~ curiosity)는 several benefits를 후치수식하는 현재분사이다.
- include는 동명사를 목적어로 취하는 3형식 동사이다.

VOCA
including ~를 포함하는

053 In the near future, I <u>believe that most people will wear user-friendly equipment making their daily lives even more convenient.</u>

> **해석** 가까운 미래에, 나는 대부분의 사람들이 일상을 훨씬 더 편하게 만들어 주는 사용자 친화적인 장치를 입을 것이라고 믿는다.

KILLER
- believe [that + 완] : ~라고 믿는다
- (making ~ convenient)는 user-friendly equipment를 후치수식하는 현재분사이다.
- make + N + 형용사 : (명사)를 (형용사)하게 만들다
- even은 비교급을 강조한다.

054 To say that we should try to be a better person <u>does not necessarily mean that we have to curb our anger all the time.</u>

> **해석** 우리가 더 나은 사람이 되려고 노력해야 한다고 말하는 것이 언제나 분노를 억제해야 한다는 것을 의미하는 것은 아니다.

KILLER
- say [that + 완] : ~라고 말하다
- not necessarily 항상 ~한 것은 아니다
- mean [that + 완] : ~를 의미하다

VOCA
curb 억제하다, 제한하다
all the time 항상(= always)

055 This result <u>moved that a policy maker be concerned with the cultural context.</u>

> **해석** 이 결과는 정책 입안자가 문화적 배경에 관심을 가져야 한다고 제안했다.

KILLER
move [that + 완] : ~해야 한다고 주장하다 (주요명제 → 동사원형 be)

VOCA
policy maker 정책 입안자
be concerned with ~와 관련 있다, 관심 있다
context 배경, 맥락, 문맥

056 Asked to <u>recall what they had seen</u>, they remembered only negative things about the incident.

> **해석** 그들이 보았던 것을 기억해 보라는 요청을 받았을 때, 그들은 그 사건에 대해 부정적인 것들만 기억했다.

KILLER
- recall [what + 불] : ~를 기억해내다
- ask A to V : A가 V하도록 요구하다, 요청하다

VOCA
recall 기억해내다
(= remember, recollect)
incident 사건

〈3형식 동사 + if/whether 목적어〉

057 Even after being invited, I stayed suspicious and asked again and again whether there was any mistake.

058 I was wondering if it would be convenient for you to see me on Monday.

> (2) 4형식

059 She also gave Betty two months' salary as severance pay.

060 A powerful flashlight showed the child the end of the cave.

061 Natural selection has allowed us the ability to feel pity for someone who is suffering.

062 Altruism has always existed, but the Internet gives it a stepping stone where it can have a significant impact on the globe.

057 Even after being invited, I stayed suspicious and asked again and again whether there was any mistake.

해석 : 심지어 초대를 받은 이후에도, 나는 의심하는 상태를 유지하면서 계속해서 실수가 있는지 아닌지를 물었다.
KILLER :
- ask [whether S + V] : ~인지 아닌지 묻다, 질문하다
- 2형식 stay + 형용사

058 I was wondering if it would be convenient for you to see me on Monday.

해석 : 네가 월요일에 나를 만나는 것이 편할지가 궁금하다.
KILLER :
- wonder [if S + V] : ~인지 아닌지 궁금하다
- 부정사 앞에 쓰인 for N는 의미상의 주어이다.

059 She also gave Betty two months' salary as severance pay.

해석 : 그녀는 또한 Betty에게 두 달 치 월급을 퇴직금으로 주었다.
KILLER :
4형식 give

VOCA
severance pay 퇴직금, 퇴직 수당

060 A powerful flashlight showed the child the end of the cave.

해석 : 강력한 손전등이 아이들에게 동굴의 끝 부분을 보여 주었다.
KILLER :
4형식 show

061 Natural selection has allowed us the ability to feel pity for someone who is suffering.

해석 : 자연 선택은 우리에게 고통스러워하는 누군가에 대해 동정심을 느낄 수 있는 능력을 허락했다.
KILLER :
4형식 allow

VOCA
pity 연민, 동정심
suffer (from) 고통을 받다, 시달리다

062 Altruism has always existed, but the Internet gives it a stepping stone where it can have a significant impact on the globe.

해석 : 이타주의는 언제나 존재했으나, 인터넷은 그것이 전 세계에 상당한 영향력을 가질 수 있는 디딤돌을 제공했다.
KILLER :
4형식 give

VOCA
altruism 이타심
stepping stone 디딤돌
globe 지구, 세계

063 In one study, researchers gave happily married women moderately painful shocks to their ankles.

> (3) 5형식 leave, keep, find

064 Raspberries can keep your heart strong.

065 Although begging for money to keep himself warm and fed, he liked his carefree life.

066 Even an hour alone in the tub with a good book can make you emotionally relaxed.

067 The rabbit makes the chase more difficult and tiring for the coyote.

068 Others reject a chance to study abroad because they don't consider themselves adventurous enough.

063 In one study, researchers gave happily married women moderately painful shocks to their ankles.

[해석] 한 연구에서, 연구원들은 행복한 기혼 여성들의 발목에 적당히 고통스러운 충격을 주었다.
[KILLER]
- 4형식 give
- 부사 + 형용사 + 명사 : happily married women, moderately painful shocks

[VOCA]
married 결혼한, 기혼의
moderately 적당한, 알맞게

064 Raspberries can keep your heart strong.

[해석] 산딸기는 심장을 건강하게 해준다.
[KILLER]
5형식 keep

065 Although begging for money to keep himself warm and fed, he liked his carefree life.

[해석] 비록 자신을 따뜻하게 하고 먹여 살리기 위해 돈을 구걸했지만, 그는 그의 태평스러운 삶을 좋아했다.
[KILLER]
5형식 keep

[VOCA]
fed 배부른 (feed – fed – fed : (타) 먹이를 주다)
carefree 근심 없는, 태평한

066 Even an hour alone in the tub with a good book can make you emotionally relaxed.

[해석] 좋은 책이 있는 욕조에서 혼자 한 시간만 있어도 정서적으로 여유가 생길 수 있다.
[KILLER]
5형식 make

[VOCA]
tub 통, 욕조

067 The rabbit makes the chase more difficult and tiring for the coyote.

[해석] 토끼는 코요테가 쫓는 것을 더 힘들고 지치게 만든다.
[KILLER]
- 5형식 make
- 감정분사 tiring은 the chase를 수식한다.

[VOCA]
chase 추적(하다)

068 Others reject a chance to study abroad because they don't consider themselves adventurous enough.

[해석] 다른 사람들은 스스로가 충분히 모험적이라고 생각하지 않기 때문에 해외에서 공부할 기회를 거부한다.
[KILLER]
- 5형식 consider
- 주어와 목적어가 같은 경우 목적어 자리에는 재귀대명사(themselves)를 써야 한다.
- 형/부 + enough : 부사 enough는 후치수식한다.

[VOCA]
reject 거부하다
adventurous 모험을 즐기는

069 The very act of resisting temptations eats up concentration and leaves you mentally exhausted.

070 Internet provides companies with the ability to make real-time data widely available.

071 If lawmakers changed policies of the government too frequently, people might find their government whimsical and unreliable.

072 Highly civilized people might find it possible to live amicably together without laws, for they would rely on good sense to solve their problems.

(4) 5형식 think, believe, consider

073 We thought him as one of the richest men in Europe.

074 She thought transporting goods by rail rather than by road to be better.

내 인생 마지막 기본 영어구문

069 The very act of resisting temptations eats up concentration and <u>leaves</u> <u>you</u> <u>mentally exhausted</u>.

[해석] 유혹에 저항하는 바로 그 행동이 네 집중력을 소모시키고 정신적으로 지치게 만든다.
[KILLER]
- 5형식 leave
- 감정분사 exhausted는 you를 수식한다.

VOCA
the very 바로 그
eat up (1) 사로잡다
(2) 잡아먹다, 먹어치우다

070 Internet provides companies with the ability to <u>make</u> <u>real-time data</u> <u>widely available</u>.

[해석] 인터넷은 회사들에게 실시간 데이터를 널리 이용할 수 있는 능력을 제공한다.
[KILLER]
- 5형식 make
- provide A with B : A에게 B를 제공하다

VOCA
realtime 실시간
available 사용/구입 가능한

071 If lawmakers changed policies of the government too frequently, people might <u>find</u> <u>their government</u> <u>whimsical and unreliable</u>.

[해석] 만약 입법자들이 그들 정부의 정책을 너무 자주 바꾼다면, 사람들은 그들의 정부가 변덕스러우며 의지할 만하지 않다고 생각했을 텐데.
[KILLER]
- 5형식 find
- 가정법 과거 (If S 과거동사, S might RV)

VOCA
whimsical (1) 엉뚱한, 기발한
(2) 변덕스러운
(= changeable, fickle, capricious)
unreliable 믿을 수 없는

072 Highly civilized people might <u>find</u> <u>it</u> <u>possible</u> to live amicably together without laws, for they would rely on good sense to solve their problems.

[해석] 고도로 문명화된 사람들은 법이 없어도 우호적으로 함께 사는 것이 가능할지도 모르는데, 그들은 그들의 문제를 풀기 위해 상식에 의존할 것이기 때문이다.
[KILLER]
5형식 find (가목적어 it - 진목적어 to V)

VOCA
highly 고도로
civilized 문명화된
amicably 우호적으로
good sense 상식

073 We <u>thought</u> <u>him</u> <u>as one of the richest men</u> in Europe.

[해석] 우리는 그를 유럽에서 가장 부유한 사람 중 한 명으로 생각했다.
[KILLER]
- 5형식 think
- one of 복수명사

074 She <u>thought</u> transporting goods by rail rather than by road to be better.

[해석] 그녀는 도로보다는 철도로 화물을 운송하는 것이 더 나을 거라고 생각했다.
[KILLER]
- 5형식 think
- A rather than B : B라기보다는 A

VOCA
goods 물건

075 Some think the birds to be good omens.

076 I believe her to be a very loving and patient woman.

077 I consider your action to be very irresponsible.

078 I don't consider it desirable for you to go there alone.

079 Many people who love reading believe the most interesting literature written today to be nonfiction.

내 인생 **마지막 기본 영어구문**

075 Some think the birds to be good omens.

> 해석 : 어떤 사람들은 그 새가 좋은 징조라고 생각한다.
> KILLER
> 5형식 think

VOCA
omen 징조, 조짐

076 I believe her to be a very loving and patient woman.

> 해석 : 나는 그녀가 매우 다정하고 인내심 있는 여자라고 믿는다.
> KILLER
> 5형식 believe

VOCA
loving 다정한(= affectionate, tender)
patient (명) 환자
 (형) 참을성 있는, 인내심 있는

077 I consider your action to be very irresponsible.

> 해석 : 나는 너의 행동이 매우 무책임하다고 생각한다.
> KILLER
> 5형식 consider

078 I don't consider it desirable for you to go there alone.

> 해석 : 나는 네가 거기에 혼자 가는 것이 바람직하다고 생각하지 않는다.
> KILLER
> 5형식 consider

VOCA
desirable 바람직한

079 Many people who love reading believe the most interesting literature written today to be nonfiction.

> 해석 : 독서를 사랑하는 많은 사람들은 오늘날 쓰인 가장 흥미로운 문학은 논픽션이라고 믿는다.
> KILLER
> 5형식 believe

Chapter 02 여러 가지 동사의 모습 파악하기 **101**

(5) 일반 5형식 동사와 사역동사, 준사역동사, 지각동사

〈일반 5형식 동사〉

080 The general ordered his men to cease fire.

081 Cotton clothing allows your skin to breathe.

082 We have long persuaded her to confess her crimes.

083 The scientists are encouraging more people to protect several species that live in the oceans.

084 The doctor allows his patients to make an informed decision based on their own health conditions.

085 On the first day of class, students expect their professors to give an overview of the course.

086 The pressure from your foot would cause the sand to act more like a liquid, and you'd sink right in.

080 The general ordered his men to cease fire.

해석 그 장군은 부하들에게 사격 중지를 명령했다.
KILLER
5형식 order A to V (A가 V하도록 명령하다)

VOCA
cease fire 사격을 중지하다

081 Cotton clothing allows your skin to breathe.

해석 면직물은 피부가 호흡을 할 수 있게 해 준다.
KILLER
5형식 allow A to V (A가 V하도록 설득하다)

082 We have long persuaded her to confess her crimes.

해석 우리는 오랫동안 그녀에게 범행을 자백하라고 설득했다.
KILLER
5형식 persuade A to V (A가 V하도록 설득하다)

VOCA
confess 자백하다, 고백하다

083 The scientists are encouraging more people to protect several species that live in the oceans.

해석 과학자들은 더 많은 사람들이 바다에 사는 몇몇 종을 보호하도록 권장하고 있다.
KILLER
5형식 encourage A to V (A가 V하도록 격려하다)

084 The doctor allows his patients to make an informed decision based on their own health conditions.

해석 의사는 환자가 자신의 건강 상태에 따라 현명한 결정을 내릴 수 있게 해준다.
KILLER
5형식 allow A to V (A가 V하도록 허락하다)

VOCA
make a decision 판단하다
informed 현명한
based on ~에 기반하여, ~에 따라

085 On the first day of class, students expect their professors to give an overview of the course.

해석 수업 첫날, 학생들은 교수님이 그 과정에 대한 개요를 말해주기를 기대한다.
KILLER
5형식 expect A to V (A가 V하기를 기대/예상하다)

VOCA
overview 개관, 개요

086 The pressure from your foot would cause the sand to act more like a liquid, and you'd sink right in.

해석 당신의 발에서 나오는 압력은 모래가 더 액체처럼 움직이게 만들 것이고, 당신은 바로 가라앉게 될 것이다.
KILLER
5형식 cause A to V (A가 V하도록 유발하다/만들다)

VOCA
sink 가라앉다

087 Researchers asked back pain patients to rate their degree of disability and report how much pain they had while lying in bed and rising in the morning.

088 The knowledge gained by a practical experience of the operation of the machine enables me to affirm that there is no genuine economical advantage in the use of this ingenious article.

⟨사역동사 make, have, let⟩

089 The comedian made the audience laugh constantly.

090 Henry looked exhausted, so I had him pack up his books and go to bed.

091 I had to yell to make myself heard over the noise of the crowd.

092 There is no free lunch: doing one thing makes us sacrifice other opportunities.

087 Researchers asked back pain patients to rate their degree of disability and report how much pain they had while lying in bed and rising in the morning.

해석 전문가들은 요통 환자들이 어느 정도 불편한지 평가하고 잠자리에 들 때와 아침에 일어날 때에 얼마나 큰 고통을 느끼는지 보고하도록 요청했다.

KILLER
- 5형식 ask A to V (A가 V하도록 요청하다)
- 부정사에 이어지는 동사원형 rate와 report가 병치된 문장이다.

VOCA
rate (명) 속도, 비율
　　　(동) 평가하다
degree 정도, 각도, 온도, 학위
disability 장애, 불편함
report 알리다, 신고하다, 보도하다

088 The knowledge gained by a practical experience of the operation of the machine enables me to affirm that there is no genuine economical advantage in the use of this ingenious article.

해석 실제 기계 작동 경험을 통해 얻어진 지식은 내가 이 독창적인 물건의 이용에 진정한 경제적 이점은 없다는 것을 확신하게 만들었다.

KILLER
- 5형식 enable A to V (A가 V하게 만들다, 가능하게 하다)
- gained ~ machine은 주어인 the knowledge를 후치수식하는 분사이다.
- there be no 명사 : (명사)가 없다

VOCA
practical 실제의, 현실적인
affirm 단언하다, 확신하다
genuine 진정한
ingenious 독창적인, 정교한
article 물건

089 The comedian made the audience laugh constantly.

해석 그 코미디언은 끊임없이 청중을 웃게 만들었다.

KILLER
사역동사 make

VOCA
constantly 계속해서, 끊임없이
(= ceaselessly, unceasingly)

090 Henry looked exhausted, so I had him pack up his books and go to bed.

해석 헨리는 지쳐 보였고, 그래서 나는 그가 책가방을 싸고 잠자리에 들게 만들었다.

KILLER
사역동사 have

VOCA
exhausted 지친
go to bed 잠자리에 들다

091 I had to yell to make myself heard over the noise of the crowd.

해석 나는 사람들의 소음을 넘어서 내 목소리가 들리도록 만들기 위해 소리를 질러야만 했다.

KILLER
사역동사 make

VOCA
yell 소리를 지르다
crowd 대중, 사람들

092 There is no free lunch: doing one thing makes us sacrifice other opportunities.

해석 공짜 점심은 없다: 한 가지 일을 하는 것은 우리가 다른 기회를 희생하게 만든다.

KILLER
사역동사 make

VOCA
sacrifice 희생하다

093 Sometimes it feels like the world is a more dangerous place than it really is. That is because television focuses mainly on the news that made the world seem like a more dangerous place.

094 We often let emotion affect our judgement.

095 The first priority is to let those in need know that you actually care about them.

096 People seldom let their wants and needs be known because they are afraid of being turned away.

〈준사역동사 get, help〉

097 Good hygiene helps minimize the risk of infection.

098 This ointment will help to heal your cuts and scratches.

내 인생 마지막 기본 영어구문

093 Sometimes it feels like the world is a more dangerous place than it really is. That is because television focuses mainly on the news that made the world seem like a more dangerous place.

해석 때때로 세상은 실제보다 더 위험한 곳처럼 느껴진다. 그 이유는 TV가 세상이 더 위험한 것처럼 보이게 만드는 뉴스에 주로 집중하기 때문이다.

KILLER
- 사역동사 make
- like가 '마치 ~한 것처럼'이라고 해석된다면 접속사로 쓰일 수 있다.
- that ~ place는 the news를 수식하는 주격 관계대명사절이다.

VOCA
focus on 집중하다
seem like ~처럼 보이다
feel like ~처럼 느껴지다

094 We often let emotion affect our judgement.

해석 우리는 종종 감정이 우리의 판단에 영향을 미치도록 만든다.
KILLER
사역동사 let

VOCA
judgement 판단

095 The first priority is to let those in need know that you actually care about them.

해석 첫 번째 우선순위는 도움이 필요한 사람들에게 당신이 그들을 실제로 걱정하고 있다는 것을 알리는 것이다.
KILLER
사역동사 let

VOCA
those in need 가난한/어려움에 빠진/도움이 필요한 사람들
care about 마음을 쓰다, 관심을 가지다

096 People seldom let their wants and needs be known because they are afraid of being turned away.

해석 사람들은 외면당하는 것을 두려워하기 때문에 그들의 욕구나 필요가 (타인에게) 알려지도록 만들지 않는다.
KILLER
사역동사 let

VOCA
be afraid of ~를 두려워하다

097 Good hygiene helps minimize the risk of infection.

해석 청결한 위생 상태는 감염의 위험을 최소화하는 데 도움이 된다.
KILLER
준사역동사 help (minimize = to minimize)

VOCA
hygiene 위생
minimize 최소화시키다(↔ maximize)

098 This ointment will help to heal your cuts and scratches.

해석 이 연고는 베이고 긁힌 상처 치료에 도움이 된다.
KILLER
준사역동사 help (to heal = heal)

VOCA
ointment 연고
cut (베인) 상처, 자상

099 Spending a few years working in a variety of cities is going to help Frank to broaden his horizons.

100 Language helps people shape the way they think about their surrounding environment.

101 Just bring a copy to your appointment and we will get experts to analyze the data.

102 Remember to get your passport renewed in time.

103 I came to accept the idea that to get different tasks done, I should build a new machine.

099　Spending a few years working in a variety of cities is going to help Frank to broaden his horizons.

VOCA
broad 넓은 → broaden 넓히다
horizon 수평선, 시야

해석 : 다양한 도시에서 일을 하며 몇 년을 보낸 것은 그의 시야를 넓히는 데 도움이 될 것이다.

KILLER
- 준사역동사 help (to broaden = broaden)
- 동명사주어(Spending ~ of cities) 단수 취급(is going to V)
- a few + 복수명사 (약간의)
- a variety of + 복수명사 (다양한)

100　Language helps people shape the way they think about their surrounding environment.

VOCA
surrounding environment 주변 환경

해석 : 언어는 사람들이 자기의 주변 환경에 대해 생각하는 방식을 형성하는 데 도움이 된다.

KILLER
- 준사역동사 help (shape = to shape)
- the way 뒤에는 how가 생략된 형태로, 완벽한 문장이 이어진다.

101　Just bring a copy to your appointment and we will get experts to analyze the data.

VOCA
copy 복사본, (책이나 신문의) 한 부
analyze 분석하다

해석 : 약속에 사본을 가지고 와라, 그러면 우리는 전문가들이 자료를 분석하도록 할 것이다.

KILLER
준사역동사 get

102　Remember to get your passport renewed in time.

VOCA
renew 갱신하다
in time 제때에, 늦지 않게

해석 : 제때에 여권을 갱신하는 것을 잊지 말아라.

KILLER
- 준사역동사 get
- remember to V (앞으로 ~할 것을 기억하다)

103　I came to accept the idea that to get different tasks done, I should build a new machine.

해석 : 나는 다양한 일을 끝내기 위해서는, 새로운 기계를 만들 필요가 있다는 생각을 받아들이게 되었다.

KILLER
- 준사역동사 get
- come to V : ~하게 되다
- the idea + 동격의 that + 완벽한 문장 (~라는 생각)

⟨지각동사⟩

104 She saw herself smile in the mirror.

105 I saw him make a call shortly before he died.

106 I've never heard him raise his voice.

107 We were about to hear his deep warm voice filling the hall.

108 We heard unanimous concern about this matter voiced at every meeting we held.

109 He has the personality to watch others praised without feeling any unhappiness.

104 She saw herself smile in the mirror.

해석 그녀는 스스로가 거울 속에서 웃고 있는 것을 보았다.
KILLER
- 5형식 지각동사 see (smile = smiling)
- 주어와 목적어가 같은 사람이기 때문에 목적어 자리에는 재귀대명사가 필요하다.

105 I saw him make a call shortly before he died.

해석 나는 그가 죽기 직전에 전화하는 것을 보았다.
KILLER
5형식 지각동사 see (make = making)

VOCA
make a call 전화하다
shortly before ~하기 직전에

106 I've never heard him raise his voice.

해석 나는 그가 갑자기 언성을 높이는 것을 들어본 적이 없다.
KILLER
- 5형식 지각동사 hear (raise = raising)
- 타동사 raise는 이하에 목적어가 필요하고, 이 자리에 자동사 rise는 불가능하다.
- have never p.p : ~한 적 없다

107 We were about to hear his deep warm voice filling the hall.

해석 우리는 그의 깊고 따뜻한 목소리가 홀을 가득 채우는 것을 듣기 직전이었다.
KILLER
- 5형식 지각동사 hear (filling = fill)
- be about to V : ~하기 직전이다, 막 ~하려 하다

108 We heard unanimous concern about this matter voiced at every meeting we held.

해석 우리가 개최한 모든 회의에서 이 문제에 대한 만장일치의 우려가 표현되는 것을 들었다.
KILLER
- 5형식 지각동사 hear
- every + 단수명사
- meeting 뒤에는 목적격 관계대명사가 생략되어 있다.

VOCA
voice (명) 목소리
　　　(동) 목소리를 내다, 표현하다
unanimous 만장일치의
hold (1) 잡다
　　　(2) 가지다
　　　(3) 개최하다
　　　(4) 주장하다
　　　(5) (인원을) 수용하다

109 He has the personality to watch others praised without feeling any of unhappiness.

해석 그는 타인이 칭찬받는 것을 조금의 불행함도 없이 지켜보는 성격이다.
KILLER
5형식 지각동사 watch

110 She could feel the sweat run down her face and neck.

111 Drinking wine on a ship, he saw the moon reflected in the river.

112 A similar phenomenon takes place when a person watches someone experiencing an emotion and feels the same in response.

113 I observed a group of teenagers from our neighborhood conduct a peaceful protest in front of your plant.

내 인생 마지막 기본 영어구문

110 She could feel the sweat run down her face and neck.

해석: 그녀는 얼굴과 목에 땀이 흘러내리는 것을 느낄 수 있었다.
KILLER
5형식 지각동사 feel (run = running)

VOCA
sweat 땀

111 Drinking wine on a ship, he saw the moon reflected in the river.

해석: 배에서 와인을 마시면서 그는 강에 비친 달을 보았다.
KILLER
5형식 지각동사 see

VOCA
reflect 반사하다, 비추다

112 A similar phenomenon takes place when a person watches someone experiencing an emotion and feels the same in response.

해석: 어떤 사람이 누군가가 어떤 감정을 경험하는 것을 보고, 그에 대한 반응으로 같은 감정을 느낄 때 비슷한 현상은 일어난다.
KILLER
• 5형식 지각동사 watch (experiencing = experience)
• when절의 동사는 watches와 feels로 두개가 병치되어 있다.

VOCA
in response 그에 대한 반응으로
phenomenon 현상
take place 발생하다

113 I observed a group of teenagers from our neighborhood conduct a peaceful protest in front of your plant.

해석: 나는 우리 동네의 한 무리의 청소년들이 너희 공장 앞에서 평화 시위를 하는 것을 보았다.
KILLER
5형식 지각동사 observe (conduct = conducting)

VOCA
observe (1) 관찰하다
         (2) 준수하다
(= abide by, conform to, comply with)

3 시제 × 태

(1) have p.p (완료시제)

114 I have paid taxes for 3 years.

115 There had been some violence after the match, but the police are now in control of the situation.

116 Over the years, many a scholar known as alchemists has sought a mystical substance called the philosopher's stone.

117 In the past 50 years, pesticide use has increased ten times while crop losses from pest damage have doubled.

118 He told me that his aunt had bought him a pair of shoes that were the wrong size for him.

119 DDT is known as a relatively safe and extremely effective pesticide that developed countries have already used to combat malaria.

114 I have paid taxes for 3 years.

> 해석 : 나는 거의 3년 동안 세금을 냈다.
> 참고 :
> I should have paid taxes 3 years ago. (조동사 have p.p = 과거)

115 There had been some violence after the match, but the police are now in control of the situation.

> 해석 : 경기가 끝난 뒤 폭력 사태가 있었지만, 지금은 경찰이 상황을 통제하고 있다.
> KILLER :
> the police는 복수 취급된다.

VOCA
violence 폭행, 폭력사태
be in control 통제하다

116 Over the years, many a scholar known as alchemists has sought a mystical substance called the philosopher's stone.

> 해석 : 수년간, 연금술사라고 알려져 있는 많은 학자들은 현자의 돌이라고 불리는 신화적인 물건을 찾아왔다.
> KILLER :
> • many a 단수명사 + 단수동사
> • (known as alchemists)는 a scholar을 후치수식하는 분사이고,
> • (called the philosopher's stone)은 a mystical substance를 후치수식하는 분사이다.

VOCA
scholar 학자
alchemist 연금술사

117 In the past 50 years, pesticide use has increased ten times while crop losses from pest damage have doubled.

> 해석 : 지난 50년 동안 해충제 사용은 10배 증가한 반면 해충 피해로 인한 농작물 손실은 2배 증가했다.

VOCA
pesticide use 해충제 사용
crop loss 농작물 손실
pest damage 해충 피해

118 He told me that his aunt had bought him a pair of shoes that were the wrong size for him.

> 해석 : 그는 내게 고모가 자신에게 맞지 않는 크기의 신발 한 켤레를 사줬다고 말했다.
> KILLER :
> • 이 문장에서 had p.p는 대과거로, told보다 더 이전에 발생한 일을 나타낸다.
> • tell은 사람목적어를 취할 수 있으나, say는 그렇지 않다.

119 DDT is known as a relatively safe and extremely effective pesticide that developed countries have already used to combat malaria.

> 해석 : DDT는 선진국이 말라리아를 정복하기 위해 이미 사용한 비교적 안전하고 매우 효과적인 살충제라고 알려져 있다.
> KILLER :
> • have already p.p : 이미 ~했다
> • be known as(~로 알려져 있다) vs. be known for(~로 유명하다)
> • pesticide 뒤의 that은 목적격 관계대명사로, 생략 가능하다.

VOCA
relatively 비교적
pesticide 살충제
developed countries 선진국
combat 싸우다, 물리치다
developing countries
후진국, 개발도상국

120 I am delighted to learn that your team's advertising campaign has just won the Advertisement of the Year Award.

121 People want to feel special, which is a normal human desire, and I have never met a person who doesn't appreciate this kind of attention.

122 In addition, they said that it would be much more difficult to revive the genes of dinosaurs, which have been extinct for millions of years.

(2) be p.p (수동태)

〈3형식 수동태 : be p.p〉

123 The wilderness preserve owned by the town was largely destroyed.

124 Such sounds are comparatively clear when they are carried through the earth.

125 The true size of his fortune is calculated not by what he keeps but by what he gives.

120 I am delighted to learn that your team's advertising campaign has just won the Advertisement of the Year Award.

[해석] 귀하 팀의 광고 캠페인이 최근 '올해의 광고상'을 수상했다는 것을 알게 되어 기쁩니다.
[KILLER]
have just p.p : 방금/막 ~했다

121 People want to feel special, which is a normal human desire, and I have never met a person who doesn't appreciate this kind of attention.

[해석] 사람들은 (스스로가) 특별하다고 느끼길 바라는데, 그것은 평범한 인간의 욕망이고, 나는 이런 종류의 관심을 고마워하지 않는 사람을 만난 적이 없다.
[KILLER]
- have never p.p : ~한 적 없다
- who는 주격관계대명사이므로 뒤에 동사가 이어지고, 이 동사는 선행사에 수일치되어야 한다.

[VOCA]
appreciate (1) 인정하다
(2) 인식하다, 식별하다
(3) 감사하다
(4) 감상하다

122 In addition, they said that it would be much more difficult to revive the genes of dinosaurs, which have been extinct for millions of years.

[해석] 또한 그들은 수백만 년 동안 멸종 상태였던 공룡의 유전자를 되살리는 것이 훨씬 더 어려울 것이라고 말했다.
[KILLER]
- it은 가주어, to revive ~ dinosaurs는 진주어로 쓰였다.
- much는 비교급 강조 부사이므로 이 자리에 very, too, so는 쓰일 수 없다.
- 문장에 선표현인 for millions of years가 쓰였으므로, 완료시제 have been이 필요하다.

[VOCA]
revive 부활시키다, 되살리다
extinct 멸종한
millions of 수백만의

123 The wilderness preserve owned by the town was largely destroyed.

[해석] 마을에 의해 소유된 야생 보호 구역은 대부분 파괴되었다.
[KILLER]
p.p (형용사) vs. be p.p (수동태) : 같은 수동이라도 (1) 명사를 꾸미는 준동사 자리에는 p.p, (2) 문장의 본동사 자리에는 be p.p가 쓰이게 된다.

[VOCA]
preserve (동) 보호하다, 지키다
(명) 보호구역, 보존제
largely 대체로, 부분

124 Such sounds are comparatively clear when they are carried through the earth.

[해석] 그러한 소리는 땅을 통해 운반될 때 비교적 선명하다.
[KILLER]
such는 형용사이므로 명사인 sounds를 수식할 수 있다. (so 부사 vs. such 형용사)

[VOCA]
comparatively 비교적으로
earth (1) 지구 (2) 땅

125 The true size of his fortune is calculated not by what he keeps but by what he gives.

[해석] 그의 재산의 진정한 크기는 그가 무엇을 가지고 있느냐가 아니라 무엇을 주느냐에 따라 계산된다.
[KILLER]
not A but B : A가 아니라 B

[VOCA]
fortune (1) 운 (2) 재산

⟨4형식 수동태 : be p.p + 명사⟩

126 Patients are taught how to control their diet.

127 He was asked the same question so many times that the answer became mechanical.

128 As a reward for participating in the study, the subjects were told that they could have the record of their choice.

129 When the Olympics returned to Greece in 2004, every medal winner was given an olive wreath along with their medal.

⟨5형식 수동태 (1) : be p.p + 형용사⟩

130 Golden poison frogs are considered poisonous.

131 Most of the hostages are kept safe and will be reunited with their families soon.

126 Patients are taught how to control their diet.

해석 환자들은 어떻게 식단을 조절하는지를 배운다.
KILLER
[how to V (어떻게 V하는지)] = 명사

127 He was asked the same question so many times that the answer became mechanical.

해석 그는 같은 질문을 너무 많이 받아서 대답이 기계적일 정도였다.
KILLER
so 형/부 that S + V : 너무 (형/부)해서 (S + V)할 정도이다

128 As a reward for participating in the study, the subjects were told that they could have the record of their choice.

해석 연구에 참여한 것에 대한 보상으로, 피실험자들은 그들이 선택한 기록을 가질 수 있다고 들었다.
KILLER
participate는 대표적인 자동사이므로 the study 앞에 전치사가 필요하다.

129 When the Olympics returned to Greece in 2004, every medal winner was given an olive wreath along with their medal.

해석 2004년 올림픽이 그리스로 돌아왔을 때 (다시 그리스에서 열렸을 때), 모든 메달 수상자들은 메달과 함께 월계관을 받았다.
KILLER
• 종속절이 when S + 과거동사이므로, 주절에도 단순과거시제가 적절하다.
• every 단수명사 + 단수동사

VOCA
olive wreath 월계관
along with ~와 함께

130 Golden poison frogs are considered poisonous.

해석 금빛 독개구리는 독이 있는 것으로 여겨진다.
KILLER
5형식 consider + 명사 + (as) 명/형

131 Most of the hostages are kept safe and will be reunited with their families soon.

해석 대부분의 인질들은 안전하게 지켜지고 있으며 곧 가족들과 재회할 것이다.
KILLER
• 5형식 keep + 명사 + 형용사
• 주어가 〈부분(most) of 명사〉인 경우, 명사가 동사의 수를 결정한다.
• 문장의 동사는 are kept와 will be reunited 두 가지이고, and로 병치되어 있다.

VOCA
hostage 인질
reunite 재회하다, 재결합하다

132 Many foods, such as meat, canned vegetables and soups, are made available in low-fat versions.

133 Elderly people are not left lonely in their own homes but made to get out and socialize.

〈5형식 수동태 (2): be p.p + to V〉

134 Locals were told to evacuate.

135 Children are taught to respect different cultures.

136 We were requested to assemble in the lobby.

137 The first group was shown a video and then asked to imagine that situation.

138 In one study, subjects listened to four music records and were asked to rate how much they liked each one.

132 Many foods, such as meat, canned vegetables and soups, are made available in low-fat versions.

해석 고기, 통조림 야채, 수프와 같은 많은 음식들이 저지방 버전으로 제공되었다.
KILLER
5형식 make + 명사 + 형용사

133 Elderly people are not left lonely in their own homes but made to get out and socialize.

해석 노인들은 자신의 집에 외롭게 남겨지지 않고 밖으로 나와 사회활동을 하게 되었다.
KILLER
5형식 leave + 명사 + 형용사

VOCA
elderly (형) 나이가 든
　　　　(old보다 정중한 표현)
lonely (형) 외로운
socialize 사람들과 사귀다, 어울리다, 사회활동을 하다

134 Locals were told to evacuate.

해석 지역 주민들은 피난을 가라는 말을 들었다.
KILLER
5형식 tell A to V

VOCA
evacuate 대피하다, 피난가다

135 Children are taught to respect different cultures.

해석 아이들은 다른 문화를 존중하라는 것을 배운다.
KILLER
5형식 teach A to V

136 We were requested to assemble in the lobby.

해석 우리는 로비에 모여 달라는 요청을 받았다.
KILLER
5형식 request A to V

VOCA
assemble ⑴ 모이다, 집합하다
　　　　　⑵ 조립하다
　　　　　　 (↔ disassemble)

137 The first group was shown a video and then asked to imagine that situation.

해석 첫 번째 그룹은 비디오를 보고 그 후에 그 상황을 상상해 보라는 요청을 받았다.
KILLER
5형식 ask A to V

138 In one study, subjects listened to four music records and were asked to rate how much they liked each one.

해석 한 연구에서, 피실험자들은 네 개의 음악 레코드를 듣고 그들이 각 레코드를 얼마나 좋아하는지 평가하도록 요청을 받았다.
KILLER
5형식 ask A to V

VOCA
rate 평가하다

139 Children who had words with their friends were made to stand at the back of the class.

140 Many conservatives urge that illegal immigrants not be allowed to apply for citizenship.

141 Hong Kong International Airport was forced to cancel flights on Monday as thousands of demonstrators crowded into the terminal. Flights have resumed, but the closure has spread jitters about travel to the popular destination.

〈조동사 be p.p〉

142 The award-winning teams will be offered the opportunity to participate in the "2025 Korean Food Festival".

143 Some genetic diseases can now be treated by replacing damaged genes with healthy ones.

139 Children who had words with their friends were made to stand at the back of the class.

해석 친구들과 말다툼을 한 아이들은 교실 맨 뒤에 서있게 된다.
KILLER
사역동사 make의 수동태 : be made to V

VOCA
have words with ~와 말다툼하다
(= quarrel, argue)

140 Many conservatives urge that illegal immigrants not be allowed to apply for citizenship.

해석 많은 보수주의자들은 불법 이민자들이 시민권을 신청하는 것을 허용받지 못해야 한다고 촉구한다.
KILLER
• 5형식 allow A to V
• urge(촉구하다)는 주요명제동사이므로 that절에 should가 생략된 동사원형이 쓰여야 한다.

VOCA
conservative 보수주의자
apply for ~에 지원하다, 신청하다

141 Hong Kong International Airport was forced to cancel flights on Monday as thousands of demonstrators crowded into the terminal. Flights have resumed, but the closure has spread jitters about travel to the popular destination.

해석 홍콩 국제공항은 월요일에 수천 명의 시위대가 터미널로 몰려듦에 따라 항공편을 취소하도록 강요받았다(취소해야만 했다). 항공편은 재개됐지만, 이번 폐쇄로 인기 여행지 여행에 대한 불안감이 확산됐다.
KILLER
5형식 force A to V

VOCA
resume 다시 시작하다, 재개되다
jitters 초조함
destination 목적지, 관광지

142 The award-winning teams will be offered the opportunity to participate in the "2025 Korean Food Festival".

해석 수상팀은 '2025 한식 페스티벌'에 참가할 수 있는 기회를 받게 될 것이다.

143 Some genetic diseases can now be treated by replacing damaged genes with healthy ones.

해석 일부 유전 질환은 손상된 유전자를 건강한 유전자로 대체함으로써 치료될 수 있다.
KILLER
• by Ving : ~함으로써
• replace A with B : A를 B로 교체하다
• ones는 genes를 대신하는 대명사이므로, 복수대명사를 써야 한다.
• damaged(손상된)는 genes를 꾸며주는 분사이다.

144 Children must be taught not to chase the wild birds as well as rabbits at the park.

145 At least 59 of those who should have been recalled to prison have committed new offences, including rape and robbery.

(3) 여러 가지 형태의 수동태

⟨have been p.p (완료시제 × 수동태)⟩

146 Promising advances have been made in the area of human genetics.

147 DNA left behind at the scene of a crime has been accepted as evidence in court.

148 Babies who have been exposed more often to salted food show a stronger preference for salted cereal.

149 Countries which have been emitting greenhouse gases for a long time will have to bear a larger share than other countries.

144 Children must be taught not to chase the wild birds as well as rabbits at the park.

[해석] 어린이들은 공원에서 토끼뿐만 아니라 야생 새도 쫓지 않도록 교육받아야 한다.

KILLER
- 준동사를 부정하는 not은 앞에 놓여야 한다.
- A as well as B : B뿐만 아니라 A도

VOCA
chase 추적하다, 뒤쫓다

145 At least 59 of those who should have been recalled to prison have committed new offences, including rape and robbery.

[해석] 교도소로 소환되었어야 할 사람 중 최소한 59명이 강간과 강도 같은 새로운 범죄를 저질렀다.

KILLER
- those who : ~한 사람들 (복수 취급 → have committed)
- should have been p.p : ~했어야 했는데.. (should have p.p) × 수동태 (be p.p)

VOCA
at least 최소한
rape and robbery 강간과 강도
recall 기억해내다, 소환하다
commit 저지르다
offence 위법행위

146 Promising advances have been made in the area of human genetics.

[해석] 인간 유전학 분야에서 유망한 발전이 있었다.

VOCA
promising 전도유망한, 긍정적인
(암기분사)

147 DNA left behind at the scene of a crime has been accepted as evidence in court.

[해석] 범죄 현장에 남겨진 DNA가 법정에서 증거로 채택됐다.

KILLER
- left ~ a crime은 과거분사(p.p)로, 주어인 DNA를 후치수식한다.
- evidence는 불가산명사이므로 an evidence, evidences 등의 표현은 옳지 않다.

VOCA
left behind 뒤처진, 남겨진
the scene of a crime 범죄 현장

148 Babies who have been exposed more often to salted food show a stronger preference for salted cereal.

[해석] 소금 간이 된 음식에 더 자주 노출된 아기들은 간이 된 시리얼에 대한 더 강한 선호도를 보인다.

VOCA
preference 선호, 취향

149 Countries which have been emitting greenhouse gases for a long time will have to bear a larger share than other countries.

[해석] 오랫동안 온실가스를 배출해 온 나라들은 다른 나라들보다 더 큰 몫을 감당해야 할 것이다.

KILLER
- have been p.p : 완료시제 × 수동태
- have been Ving : 완료진행시제 × 능동태
- for a long time이 있으므로 완료시제인 have p.p가 필요하다.
- will must는 옳지 않은 표현이고, will have to가 적절하다.
- 문장에 than other countries라는 표현이 있으므로 비교급인 larger이 적절하다.

VOCA
emit 내뿜다, 배출하다
bear a share 몫을 감당하다

⟨be being p.p (진행시제 × 수동태)⟩

150 I was vaguely conscious that I was being watched.

151 Patients were being discharged from the hospital too early.

152 Water used to maintain the hotels around the temples is being pumped from groundwater under the city.

153 If you watch airline attendants when flight safety instructions are being given, you'll notice them holding the life jacket and oxygen mask.

150   I was vaguely conscious that I was being watched.

해석 내가 감시당하고 있다는 것을 어렴풋이 알고 있었다.
KILLER
be conscious of 명사 또는 that S+V : ~를 알다, 의식하다

VOCA
vaguely 모호하게, 희미하게, 어렴풋이

151   Patients were being discharged from the hospital too early.

해석 환자들이 병원에서 너무 빨리 퇴원되고 있었다.
KILLER
too는 원급을 강조하는 부사이므로 비교급인 earlier과는 쓰이지 않는다.

VOCA
discharge (1) 배출/방출하다
(2) 해방시키다
(3) 발사하다
(4) 퇴원시키다
(5) 해고하다
(6) 석방하다
(7) (배, 비행기에서) 짐을 내리다

152   Water used to maintain the hotels around the temples is being pumped from groundwater under the city.

해석 사원들 주변의 호텔을 유지하기 위해 사용되는 물은 도시 아래의 지하수로부터 퍼 올려지고 있다.
KILLER
used to ~ temples는 water를 후치수식하는 분사이다.

153   If you watch airline attendants when flight safety instructions are being given, you'll notice them holding the life jacket and oxygen mask.

해석 기내 안전 수칙이 소개되고 있을 때 승무원을 본다면, 너는 그들이 구명조끼와 산소마스크를 들고 있는 것을 알 수 있을 것이다.
KILLER
watch나 are being given은 미래시제로 쓰일 수 없다. (시조부현미)

VOCA
airline attendant 승무원
life jacket 구명조끼

 김태은 영어

마지막 기본 영어구문

CHAPTER

03

And, Or, But은
묶거나 끊기

And, Or, But은 묶거나 끊기

(1) and, or, but + 문장

001 I think that for describing the physical means of traveling and carrying, the word 'transport' is better than communication, but I suppose both will go on being used.

002 Firm disciplines are directed toward the infant and these are not relaxed until a man runs his own life in which he gets a self-supporting job and sets up a household of his own.

003 Nevertheless, opportunities for pleasure outside of one's work were scarce and nobody in North America had a surplus of leisure before the rise of our modern mechanical civilization.

(2) and, or, but + 문장이 아닌 것

004 He wanted to encourage his son to play the piano and to do more math.

005 This physical reaction prepares the body either to fight the danger or to escape it.

006 He proved the connection between how often people used relational words and how long they lived.

내 인생 마지막 기본 영어구문

001 I think that / for describing the physical means of traveling and carrying, / the word 'transport' is better than communication, / but I suppose both will go on being used.

[해석] 물리적인 운송 수단을 설명하기 위해 / 다른 단어로 communication보다는 'transport'가 낫다고 생각하지만 / 두 단어 모두 계속해서 쓰일 것 같다.

[VOCA]
physical 물리적인
means 방법, 수단
suppose ~해도 좋다고 인정하다,
　　　　~일 것 같다

002 Firm disciplines are directed toward the infant / and these are not relaxed / until a man runs his own life / in which he gets a self-supporting job and sets up a household of his own.

[해석] 탄탄한 훈련이 아이를 향해 겨냥되고 / 이 훈련들은 완화되지 않는다 / 그가 스스로 생계를 책임지는 직업을 구하고 자기 가족을 이루며 인생을 꾸려가기까지.

[KILLER]
- not A until B : B하고 나서야 A하다
- 전치사 + which 뒤에는 완벽한 문장이 들어간다.

[VOCA]
firm 견고한, 탄탄한
self-supporting 자립하는
direct (형) 직접적인
　　　(동) 향하다, 겨냥하다,
　　　　　지휘/총괄/명령하다

003 Nevertheless, / opportunities for pleasure outside of one's work were scarce / and nobody in North America had a surplus of leisure / before the rise of our modern mechanical civilization.

[해석] 그럼에도 불구하고, / 업무 밖에서 기쁨을 얻는 기회가 부족했고 / 북아메리카에서는 그 누구도 여분으로 남아있는 여가를 갖지 않았다 / 현대 기계 문명이 등장하기 전에는.

[VOCA]
scarce 부족한
a surplus of 여분의

004 He wanted to encourage his son to play the piano and to do more math.

[해석] 그는 아들이 피아노를 치고 수학 공부를 더 하도록 격려하고 싶었다.

[KILLER]
encourage A to V (A가 V하도록 격려하다)

005 This physical reaction prepares the body either to fight the danger or to escape it.

[해석] 이 신체적 반응은 신체를 위험과 싸우거나 위험에서 벗어나는 것에 대비시킨다.

[KILLER]
either A or B (A 또는 B 둘 중 하나)

006 He proved the connection between how often people used relational words and how long they lived.

[해석] 그는 사람들이 관계성 단어를 얼마나 자주 사용했는지와 그들이 얼마나 오래 살았는지 사이의 연관성을 증명했다.

[KILLER]
between A and B (A와 B 사이)

007 One such musician was Mozart, who is acclaimed as an immortal in music but had to struggle to survive during his lifetime.

008 The fortune teller then asked the girl to pick out the pebbles that would show her fate and that of her father.

009 From this viewpoint any two machines which work in the same way or do the same kind of job are the same kind of machine even if they are made of quite different substances and operate in quite different environments.

010 Productivity increased, and an increasing number of people were needed to operate the machines and to distribute and service the new products.

07 One such musician was Mozart, who is acclaimed as an immortal in music but had to struggle to survive during his lifetime.

[해석] 그런 음악가 중 한 명이 모차르트였는데, 그는 음악에서 불멸의 존재로 칭송받지만 그의 생애 동안 살아남기 위해 고군분투해야 했다.

VOCA
acclaim 칭송하다, 칭찬하다
immortal 죽지 않는, 불멸의
struggle to V
~하기 위해 고군분투하다

008 The fortune teller then asked the girl to pick out the pebbles that would show her fate and that of her father.

[해석] 그 다음 점술가는 소녀가 그녀와 그녀의 아버지의 운명을 보여줄 조약돌을 고르라고 요구했다.

KILLER
- ask A to V (A가 V하도록 요청하다)
- the pebble 뒤의 that은 pebble을 수식하는 주격 관계대명사이다.

009 From this viewpoint / any two machines which work in the same way or do the same kind of job are the same kind of machine / even if they are made of quite different substances and operate in quite different environments.

[해석] 이러한 관점에서 같은 방식으로 작동하거나 같은 일을 처리하는 두 기계는 완전히 다른 재료로 구성되고 전혀 다른 환경에서 작동하더라도 같은 종류의 기계이다.

KILLER
- 주어는 any two machines, 동사는 are이다. 수일치에 유의해야 한다.
- machines을 수식하는 which 이하에 동사가 work or do로 병치되어 있다.

VOCA
from this viewpoint 이러한 관점에서
in the same way 같은 방식으로
even if 비록 ~하더라도
quite 꽤나

010 Productivity increased, / and an increasing number of people were needed / to operate the machines and to distribute and service the new products.

[해석] 생산성이 증가했고, 기계를 운영하고 상품을 유통시켜서 제공하기 위해 점점 더 많은 사람이 필요했다.

KILLER
- a number of 복수명사 + 복수동사 (많은)
- to V가 '~하기 위해서'라고 해석되는 경우, 이를 부정사의 부사적 용법으로 본다. 이는 품사상 부사에 가깝기 때문에 목적어 역할을 할 수 없다.

VOCA
productivity 생산성
operate 작동/가동/조작/운용하다
distribute 분배/유포/유통하다
service (동) 점검하다, 제공하다

EXERCISE

다음 문장의 옳고 그름을 판단하고, 옳지 않은 부분은 옳게 고치시오. (01~10)

01 There is measure in all natural things in their size, speed, or violent.

02 This kind of genetic tracking helps doctors to predict the likelihood of a person getting a disease and diagnosing it.

03 My son said the shoes happened to be the same size and that the boy could have them if he wanted them.

04 He has arrested by the police and taken to the station for questioning.

05 His brand is slowly but surely making a name for itself.

06 She praised you, gave you an unexpected gift, and taking the time to write you a letter.

07 Licensing protects music from being stolen and preserve both new and older music.

ANSWER

01 There is measure in all natural things in their size, speed, or violent.
정답 violent → violence
해석 모든 자연물에는 크기, 속도, 혹은 폭력성을 판단하는 기준이 있다.

VOCA
measure 기준, 척도
violence 폭력성

02 This kind of genetic tracking helps doctors to predict the likelihood of a person getting a disease and diagnosing it.
정답 diagnosing → to diagnose
해석 이런 종류의 유전자 추적은 의사들이 사람이 병에 걸릴 가능성을 예측하고 진단하는 것을 돕는다.

03 My son said (that) the shoes happened to be the same size and that the boy could have them if he wanted them.
정답 O
해석 나의 아들은 신발이 우연히 같은 사이즈라며 소년이 원한다면 신발을 가져도 된다고 말했다.
KILLER
happen to V (우연히 ~하다)

04 He has arrested by the police and taken to the station for questioning.
정답 has → was 또는 has been
해석 그는 경찰에게 체포되어 경찰서로 심문을 받으러 끌려갔다.

VOCA
questioning 질의, 심문

05 His brand is slowly but surely making a name for itself.
정답 O
해석 그의 브랜드는 느리지만 확실히 유명해지고 있다.

VOCA
make a name for oneself 유명해지다

06 She praised you, gave you an unexpected gift, and taking the time to write you a letter.
정답 taking → took
해석 그녀는 당신을 칭찬하고, 뜻밖의 선물을 주었고, 시간을 들여 당신에게 편지를 썼다.
KILLER
take time to V : 시간을 들여서 V하다

07 Licensing protects music from being stolen and preserve both new and older music.
정답 preserve → preserves
해석 라이센싱은 음악을 도난으로부터 보호하고 새 음악과 오래된 음악을 모두 보존합니다.

EXERCISE

08 Conflict is not only unavoidable but crucial for the long-term success of the relationship.

09 I was in the habit of telling people what they wanted to hear in the moment and make a promise in order to avoid a fight.

10 Your toothbrush will be capable to analyze your breath and books an appointment with your doctor if it detects the smell of lung cancer.

ANSWER

08 Conflict is not only <u>unavoidable</u> but <u>crucial</u> for the long-term success of the relationship.
- 정답 ○
- 해석 갈등은 피할 수 없을 뿐만 아니라 장기적인 관계의 성공을 위해 중요하다.

VOCA
unavoidable 불가피한, 어쩔 수 없는
crucial 중대한, 결정적인

09 I was in the habit of <u>telling</u> people what they wanted to hear in the moment and <u>make</u> a promise in order to avoid a fight.
- 정답 make → making
- 해석 나는 싸움을 피하기 위해 사람들에게 그들이 그 순간에 듣고 싶어 하는 말을 해주고 약속을 하는 버릇이 있었다.
- KILLER
  - be in the habit of Ving (~하는 습관이 있다, ~하는 버릇이 있다)
  - in order to V (~하기 위해)

10 Your toothbrush will be capable <u>to analyze</u> your breath and <u>books</u> an appointment with your doctor if it detects the smell of lung cancer.
- 정답 to analyze → of analyzing, books → booking
- 해석 여러분의 칫솔이 폐암의 냄새를 감지하면 여러분의 입 냄새를 분석하고 의사와의 예약을 잡을 수 있을 것이다.
- KILLER
  be capable of Ving = be able to V (~할 수 있다)

VOCA
appointment 약속, 예약

박문각 김태은 영어

마지막 기본 영어구문

CHAPTER

04

전치사, 접속사 해석하기

1. 결과를 나타내는 접속사
2. 시간을 나타내는 전치사와 접속사
3. 양보나 대조를 나타내는 전치사와 접속사
4. 인과를 나타내는 전치사와 접속사
5. 조건을 나타내는 전치사와 접속사
6. 목적을 나타내는 접속사

전치사, 접속사 해석하기

1 결과를 나타내는 접속사

> ① **so** 형/부 **that** S + V : 너무 (형/부)해서 S + V ~ 하다/할 정도이다
> ② **so** 형 a 명 **that** S + V : 너무 (형)한 (명사)라 S + V ~ 하다/할 정도이다
> ③ **such** a 형 명 **that** S + V : 너무 (형)한 (명사)라 S + V ~ 하다/할 정도이다

001 My legs were trembling so badly that I could hardly stand still.

002 Our technologies are so powerful that our effects on the environment are becoming even more global.

003 Some of the village girls have such a strong country accent that I could hardly communicate with them.

004 The astronomers were so impressed with the young amateur's powers of observation that they invited him to work at the observatory.

005 If a dolphin is wounded so severely that it cannot swim to the surface by itself, other dolphins group themselves under it, pushing it upward to the air.

001 My legs were trembling <u>so</u> badly / <u>that</u> I could hardly stand still.

  [해석] 다리가 너무 심하게 떨려서 / 나는 더 이상 서 있을 수 없었다.

VOCA
tremble 떨다
badly 심하게
stand still 가만히 서 있다

002 Our technologies are <u>so</u> powerful / <u>that</u> our effects on the environment are becoming even more global.

  [해석] 우리의 기술은 매우 강력해서 / 환경에 미치는 우리의 영향은 훨씬 더 세계적이게 되고 있다.

  KILLER
  • affect는 타동사, effect는 명사이다.
  • even은 비교급을 강조하는 부사이다.

003 Some of the village girls have <u>such</u> a strong country accent / <u>that</u> I could hardly communicate with them.

  [해석] 몇몇 마을 소녀들은 시골 사투리가 너무 강해서 / 나는 그들과 거의 의사소통을 할 수 없었다.

  KILLER
  • such a strong country accent = so strong a country accent
  • hardly(= not)는 부정부사이므로 couldn't hardly처럼 쓰일 수 없다. (이중부정 금지)

004 The astronomers were <u>so</u> impressed with the young amateur's powers of observation / <u>that</u> they invited him to work at the observatory.

  [해석] 천문학자들은 젊은 아마추어의 관찰력에 깊은 인상을 받아서 / 그를 천문대에서 일하도록 초대할 정도였다.

005 If a dolphin is wounded <u>so</u> severely / <u>that</u> it cannot swim to the surface by itself, / other dolphins group themselves under it, pushing it upward to the air.

  [해석] 만약 돌고래가 너무 심하게 다쳐서 / 혼자서는 수면으로 헤엄칠 수 없다면, / 다른 돌고래들은 그 아래에서 무리를 지어 공중으로 밀어 올린다.

2 시간을 나타내는 전치사와 접속사

전치사	during, in, within, for, since, before, after
접속사	while, when, until, since, as soon as, by the time, before, after

006 You'll get a warmer reception during the busy season when there's more demand.

007 Gophers eat roots and other parts of plants they encounter while digging underground.

008 Younger smartphone users have even learned the art of texting one person while they are talking to another.

006 You'll get a warmer reception / during the busy season when there's more demand.

[해석] 수요가 더 많은 성수기에는 / 더 따뜻한 환영을 받을 수 있을 것이다.

[KILLER]
(when ~ demand)는 reception을 후치수식하는 관계부사이다.

VOCA
reception (1) 접수처 (2) 환영

007 Gophers eat roots and other parts of plants they encounter / while digging underground.

[해석] 고퍼들은 땅을 파는 동안 그들이 마주치는 식물의 뿌리들과 다른 부분들을 먹는다.

[KILLER]
- they encounter 앞에는 목적격 관계대명사가 생략되어있다.
- while digging underground (분사구문) = while they dig underground

VOCA
encounter 마주치다
(= run into, run across, bump into)

008 Younger smartphone users have even learned the art of texting one person / while they are talking to another.

[해석] 젊은 스마트폰 사용자들은 심지어 그들이 다른 사람과 대화하는 동안 한 사람에게 문자를 보내는 기술을 학습해왔다.

VOCA
the art of ~라는 기술
texting 문자 보내기

3 양보나 대조를 나타내는 전치사와 접속사

전치사	despite, in spite of
접속사	though, although, even if, even though, as, while, whereas

009 Despite all your efforts to mask emotions, they will come out in some form.

010 Even if the parents stop giving their baby sugar water, she will continue to show a greater preference for it.

011 Despite the fact that these training books had not been used for some 15 years, they still had great influence over the actions of managers.

012 Fines mean legal disapproval, whereas fees are simply prices that imply no moral or legal judgement.

013 Pigs were traditionally associated with dirtiness because of their habit of rolling around in mud while cats were believed to be clean.

014 Popular as he is, the President hasn't always managed to have his own way.

내 인생 **마지막 기본 영어구문**

009 <u>Despite</u> all your efforts to mask emotions, / they will come out in some form.

해석 감정을 감추려는 당신의 모든 노력에도 불구하고, / 그것들은 어떤 형태로든 드러날 것이다.
KILLER
they가 가리키는 것은 emotions이므로 복수대명사가 옳다.

VOCA
mask 감추다

010 <u>Even if</u> the parents stop giving their baby sugar water, / she will continue to show a greater preference for it.

해석 부모가 아기에게 설탕물을 주는 것을 중단하더라도, / 그녀는 계속해서 설탕물에 대한 더 강한 선호도를 보일 것이다.
KILLER
• stop Ving (~하는 것을 멈추다, 중단하다) vs. stop to V (~하기 위해 멈추다)
• it이 가리키는 것은 sugar water이므로 단수대명사가 옳다.

VOCA
preference 선호

011 <u>Despite</u> the fact that these training books had not been used for some 15 years, / they still had great influence over the actions of managers.

해석 이 교육용 도서들은 약 15년 동안 사용되지 않았음에도 불구하고 / 여전히 관리자들의 행동에 큰 영향을 미쳤다.
KILLER
• that ~ years는 the fact를 후치수식하는 동격이다.
• 숫자 앞에 쓰인 some은 '대략'이라고 읽는다.
• influence는 명사 또는 타동사로 쓰인다.
 (had great influence over the actions = greatly influenced the actions)

012 Fines mean legal disapproval, / <u>whereas</u> fees are simply prices that imply no moral or legal judgement.

해석 벌금은 법적 비난을 의미하는 반면, / 수수료는 단순히 도덕적 또는 법적 판단을 내포하지 않는 대가이다.

VOCA
disapproval 승인하지 않음, 불만, 비난
imply 함축하다, 내포하다

013 Pigs were traditionally associated with dirtiness / <u>because of</u> their habit of rolling around in mud / <u>while</u> cats were believed to be clean.

해석 돼지는 전통적으로 진흙 속에서 뒹굴고 / 고양이는 깨끗하다고 믿었기 때문에 / 더러움과 관련이 있었다.

VOCA
be associated with ~와 관련있다
be believed to V ~라고 알려지다

014 Popular <u>as</u> he is, / the boss hasn't always managed to have his own way.

해석 그가 인기 있었음에도 불구하고, / 사장이 항상 자기 마음대로 할 수는 없었다.
KILLER
as가 '~에도 불구하고'라는 양보의 접속사로 쓰였을 때, 종속절의 주격 보어는 문장 맨 앞으로 도치될 수 있다. 이 때에 명사인 주격 보어는 무관사로 도치되어야 한다. 또한 주어 + 동사는 도치되지 않고 정치상태를 유지한다.

VOCA
have one's own way 마음대로 하다

4 인과를 나타내는 전치사와 접속사

전치사	because of, due to, owing to, thanks to, on accout of
접속사	because, as, since, now that, in that

015 We study philosophy because of the mental skills it helps us develop.

016 Because of an unexpected snowstorm that blinded the Russian army, the Swedes won.

017 Since they have very limited mobility, they only move the necessary distances to eat, passing their lives almost motionless most of the time.

018 As the earth's surface is curved, there is a path that looks longer on a flat map.

019 As parents of multiple children know, there is no one simple formula for meeting a baby's needs.

020 As the emperor's soldiers invaded, the unprepared northern tribes fled to places where Qin's army could not reach.

015 We study philosophy / because of the mental skills it helps us develop.

:해석: 그것이 우리가 개발할 수 있게 도와주는 정신력 때문에 / 우리는 철학을 공부한다.
:KILLER:
it helps us develop 앞에는 목적격 관계대명사가 생략되어 있다.

016 Because of an unexpected snowstorm that blinded the Russian army, / the Swedes won.

:해석: 러시아군의 눈을 멀게 한 예상치 못한 눈보라 때문에 / 스웨덴이 이겼다.

:VOCA:
unexpected 예상치 못한
blind 눈을 멀게 하다

017 Since they have very limited mobility, / the tribesmen only move the necessary distances to eat, / passing their lives almost motionless most of the time.

:해석: 제한된 이동성을 가지고 있었기 때문에 (이동하기가 쉽지 않았기 때문에), / 부족민들은 먹기 위해 필요한 거리만 움직였고, / 그래서 그들은 거의 움직이지 않고 그들의 삶을 보냈다.

:VOCA:
mobility 이동성, 기동성

018 As the earth's surface is curved, / there is a path that looks longer on a flat map.

:해석: 지구 표면이 곡선을 그리면서 평평한 지도에서 더 길어 보이는 길이 있다.

019 As parents of multiple children know, / there is no one simple formula for meeting a baby's needs.

:해석: 다자녀의 부모가 알고 있듯이, / 아기의 필요를 충족시키기 위한 간단한 공식은 없다.

:VOCA:
meet (1) 만나다
     (2) (기준, 필요, 욕구를) 충족시키다

020 As the emperor's soldiers invaded, / the unprepared northern tribes fled to places where Qin's army could not reach them.

:해석: 황제의 군사들이 쳐들어오자 / 미처 준비하지 못한 북방 부족들은 진의 군대가 미치지 못하는 곳으로 달아났다.

:VOCA:
unprepared 준비가 되지 않은
flee 달아나다, 도망치다 (flee-fled-fled)

5 조건을 나타내는 전치사와 접속사

전치사	considering, given
접속사	if, unless, as long as, as far as

021 A present really isn't a present unless it is wrapped in paper.

022 She tried to give me the message that nothing was off-limits for me as long as I could learn.

023 As long as the bodybuilders are properly supervised to prevent possible injury, the rewards outweigh the risks.

EXERCISE

둘 중 옳은 것을 고르시오. (01~02)

01 As adults, we can lose flexibility rather rapidly [if / unless] we make a conscious effort to maintain it.

02 [If / Unless] getting sufficient sleep, you should feel refreshed and not have trouble getting out of bed in the morning.

021 A present really isn't a present / <u>unless</u> it is wrapped in paper.

> [해석] 선물은 종이에 싸지 않으면 / 정말 선물이 아니다.

022 She tried to give me the message that nothing was off-limits for me / <u>as long as</u> I could learn.

[VOCA]
off limits 금지된, 접근 금지의

> [해석] 그녀는 내가 배울 수 있는 한 나에게 금지된 것은 아무것도 없다는 메시지를 주려고 했다.

023 <u>As long as</u> the bodybuilders are properly supervised to prevent possible injury, / the rewards outweigh the risks.

[VOCA]
outweigh ~보다 더 크다, 능가하다

> [해석] 보디빌더들이 부상을 예방할 수 있도록 적절히 감독하는 한, / 보상은 위험을 능가한다.

ANSWER

01 As adults, we can lose flexibility rather rapidly / <u>unless</u> we make a conscious effort to maintain it.

[정답] unless
[해석] 성인의 경우 유연성을 유지하기 위해 의식적으로 노력하지 않으면 오히려 빠르게 유연성을 잃을 수 있다.
[KILLER]
rather은 부사로 '오히려, 패나'라고 해석되며, 뒤에 있는 성분을 강조하는 역할을 한다.

[VOCA]
conscious 의식적인
make an effort 노력하다

02 <u>If</u> getting sufficient sleep, / you should feel refreshed and not have trouble getting out of bed in the morning.

[정답] if
[해석] 충분한 수면을 취하고 있다면, 당신은 기분이 상쾌해야 하고 아침에 침대에서 일어나는 데 어려움을 겪지 않아야 한다.
[KILLER]
have trouble (in) Ving : ~하느라 고생하다

[VOCA]
sufficient 충분한(= adequate, good)

6 목적을 나타내는 접속사

① so that S + V ~ : ~하도록 (목적), 그래서 결국 ~하다 (결과)
② lest S should RV ~ : ~하지 않도록, 할까봐

024 Educational situations were structured so that every child could be successful nearly all the time.

025 Children were told to take only one piece of candy so that there would be plenty for everyone

026 Fortunately, material survived from the nineteenth century, so that a linguist was able to help the Kaurna people start the language again.

027 Dilemma tales are like folk tales in that they are usually short, simple, and driven entirely by plot.

내 인생 **마지막 기본 영어구문**

024　Educational situations were structured / so that every child could be successful nearly all the time.

해석 : 모든 아이들이 거의 항상 성공할 수 있도록 / 교육적 상황이 구조화되어있다.
KILLER :
every + 단수명사 + 단수동사

VOCA :
structure 구조화시키다, 만들다

025　Children were told to take only one piece of candy / so that there would be plenty for everyone.

해석 : 아이들은 사탕을 한 조각만 가져가서 모든 사람이 먹을 수 있도록 하라는 이야기를 들었다.
KILLER :
5형식 tell (tell A to V)의 수동태 : be told to V

VOCA :
plenty 풍부한 양
plenty of 많은

026　Fortunately, material of the nineteenth century survived, / so that a linguist was able to explore the language again.

해석 : 운 좋게도, 19세기의 자료가 건재했고, / 그래서 언어학자들은 그 언어를 다시 연구할 수 있었다.

VOCA :
material ⑴ 직물, 천
　　　　 ⑵ 재료, 소재, 물질
　　　　 ⑶ 자료
linguist 언어학자
explore 탐구하다, 탐험하다

027　Dilemma tales are like folk tales / in that they are usually short, simple, and driven entirely by plot.

해석 : 딜레마 이야기는 대개 짧고 단순하며 줄거리에 의해 움직인다는 점에서 민담과 유사하다.

VOCA :
tale 이야기, 소설
folk tale 설화, 전설, 민담
be driven by ~에 의해 움직이다

Chapter 04 전치사, 접속사 해석하기　**151**

박문각 김태은 영어

마지막 기본 영어구문

CHAPTER

05

준동사 정복하기

1. 부정사의 여러 가지 형태
2. 부정사의 여러 가지 해석
3. 동명사의 여러 가지 형태
4. 분사구문

준동사 정복하기

1 부정사의 여러 가지 형태

① 부정사가 본동사 보다 먼저 일어난 일일 경우 to have p.p를 사용한다.
② 부정사가 수동의 의미를 나타낼 때는 to be p.p를 사용한다.

001 He ordered a strong wall to be built to keep out the northern forces.

002 As music becomes more accessible, it is increasingly easy for music to be copied.

003 Children need to be taught how to interact with animals and when to leave the animals alone.

004 The founding population of our direct ancestors is not thought to have been larger than 2,000 individuals.

005 Within five minutes, all the eggs seemed to have been found and the children were heading back to the starting line.

내 인생 마지막 기본 영어구문

001 He ordered a strong wall to be built to keep out the northern forces.

해석 : 그는 북부 세력을 막기 위해 튼튼한 성벽을 세우라고 명령했다.
KILLER
5형식 order A to V : A가 V하도록 명령하다

VOCA
keep out 막다, 차단하다
forces 세력, 병력

002 As music becomes more accessible, it is increasingly easy for music to be copied.

해석 : 음악에 더 쉽게 접근할 수 있게 됨에 따라, 음악이 복제되기 점점 더 쉬워지고 있다.
KILLER
• 2형식 become + accessible (형용사)
• it 가주어—to V 진주어

VOCA
accessible 접근가능한, 이용가능한
copy 복제하다, 복사하다

003 Children need to be taught how to interact with animals and when to leave the animals alone.

해석 : 아이들은 동물과 어떻게 교류해야 하는지, 그리고 언제 동물을 내버려 두어야 하는지를 배워야 한다.
KILLER
• 3형식 need + 부정사 목적어 (need to V : ~할 필요가 있다)
• 5형식 leave + 명사 + 형용사 : (명사)를 (형용사)하게 내버려두다
• how to V : 어떻게 ~할지, 명사 취급
• when to V : 언제 ~할지, 명사 취급

VOCA
interact with ~와 상호작용하다, 교류하다

004 The founding population of our direct ancestors is not thought to have been larger than 2,000 individuals.

해석 : 우리의 직계 조상의 초기 집단은 2,000명을 넘지 않았을 것으로 여겨진다.
KILLER
• be thought to V : ~라고 알려져 있다, 여겨지다
• 완료부정사 to have p.p

VOCA
founding population 초기 집단, 초기 개체군, 새로운 지역에 처음 정착한 개체의 수
ancestor 조상
individual 개인, 개체

005 Within five minutes, all the eggs seemed to have been found and the children were heading back to the starting line.

해석 : 5분 안에 모든 달걀이 발견된 듯했고, 아이들은 출발선으로 돌아가고 있었다.
KILLER
완료부정사의 수동형 to have been p.p

VOCA
within ~이내에
head back 되돌아가다

Chapter 05 준동사 정복하기

006 The law of the jungle has made it inevitable for intellectually prominent humans to kill animals for food, but in terms of compassion, it is very wrong for us to destroy them due to nothing but pleasure.

006 The law of the jungle has made it inevitable for intellectually prominent humans to kill animals for food, but in terms of compassion, it is very wrong for us to destroy them due to nothing but pleasure.

해석 약육강식의 법칙은 지적으로 우월한 인간이 음식을 위해 동물을 죽이는 것을 피할 수 없게 만들었으나 연민의 관점에서 보면 단지 즐거움 때문에 그들을 죽이는 것은 매우 잘못된 일이다.

KILLER
- 5형식 make + 명사 + 형용사 (inevitable)
- it 가목적어-부정사 진목적어 (to kill ~)
- 부정사의 의미상 주어 for intellectually prominent humans
- it 가주어-부정사 진주어 (to destroy ~)
- 부정사의 의미상 주어 for us
- nothing but : 겨우, 고작, 단지

VOCA
law of the jungle 정글의 법칙, 약육강식
inevitable 불가피한, 피할 수 없는
intellectually prominent 지적으로 우월한
in terms of ~의 관점에서
compassion 연민
passion 열정
destroy 죽이다, 파괴하다
due to ~ 때문에
pleasure 즐거움, 기쁨

2 부정사의 여러 가지 해석

① in order to V, so as to V : V하기 위해 (= to V)
② 형/부 enough to V : V하기에 충분히 형/부하게
③ too 형/부 to V : 너무 형/부해서 V할 수 없다
④ easy/hard/difficult/possible to V : V하기에 쉽다/어렵다/가능하다
⑤ 감정형용사 to V : V해서 (감정형용사)하다

007 It was too early in the morning for someone to be there.

008 The message itself must be powerful enough to command attention.

009 A flea is too minute for the unaided eye to perceive each part.

010 The package was strong enough to hold a lot of groceries.

011 Many of the biggest stars in sports are tough to deal with.

012 Team sports become more difficult to organize in an adult world.

내 인생 마지막 기본 영어구문

007　It was too early in the morning for someone to be there.

해석 : 누군가가 거기 있기에는 너무 이른 아침이었다.
KILLER
- 비인칭 주어 it
- too 형/부 to V (too-to 용법) : (V)하기에는 너무 (형/부)하다
- 부정사의 의미상 주어 for someone

VOCA
early in the morning 이른 아침

008　The message itself must be powerful enough to command attention.

해석 : 그 메시지 자체가 주목을 끌 만큼 충분히 강력해야 한다.
KILLER
- 재귀대명사 itself의 강조용법
- 형/부 enough to V : (V)할 정도로 충분히 (형/부)한

VOCA
command 명령하다, 지휘하다, 지배하다, (감정을) 일으키다
command attention 주의를 끌다, 관심을 끌다

009　A flea is too minute for the unaided eye to perceive each part.

해석 : 벼룩은 육안으로는 그 각 부분을 식별하기엔 너무 작다.
KILLER
- too 형/부 to V (too-to 용법) : (V)하기에는 너무 (형/부)하다
- 부정사의 의미상 주어 for the unaided eye
- each + 단수명사 : 각각의 ~(= each of the 복수명사)

VOCA
flea 벼룩
minute 분; 작은, 미세한(= fine)
unaided eye 맨눈
perceive 인식하다, 식별하다

010　The package was strong enough to hold a lot of groceries.

해석 : 그 상자는 많은 식료품을 담을 만큼 충분히 튼튼했다.
KILLER
- 형/부 enough to V : (V)할 정도로 충분히 (형/부)한
- a lot of(= lots of) + 가산명사의 복수형 또는 불가산명사

VOCA
package 소포, 포장, 포장용기
groceries 식료품

011　Many of the biggest stars in sports are tough to deal with.

해석 : 스포츠계의 가장 유명한 스타들 중 많은 이들은 다루기 힘들다.
KILLER
- hard/difficult/tough to V : ~하기에 힘든
- many of 복수명사 + 복수동사 : (명사) 중 대부분, 대부분의 (명사)

VOCA
deal with 다루다, 처리하다, 해결하다

012　Team sports become more difficult to organize in an adult world.

해석 : 성인 세계에서는 팀 스포츠를 조직하는 것이 더 어려워진다.
KILLER
2형식 become + 형용사 : ~하게 변하다, ~해지다

VOCA
organize 조직하다, 준비하다

Chapter 05 준동사 정복하기　159

013 His high school friends were amazed to hear his voice on the radio.

014 Spider plants love to absorb carbon dioxide, and they're easy to grow.

015 Suppose that you come home from school to find a cushion torn apart on the living room floor.

016 Hiding behind a barrier is a normal response we learn at an early age to protect ourselves.

017 Manufacturers will use the information generated by these smart products to sell you other services.

018 A map must distort reality in order to portray a complex, three-dimensional world on a flat sheet of paper.

013 His high school friends were amazed to hear his voice on the radio.

해석 그의 고등학교 친구들은 그의 목소리를 라디오에서 듣고 놀랐다.
KILLER
감정분사 amazed

014 Spider plants love to absorb carbon dioxide, and they're easy to grow.

해석 자주달개비는 이산화탄소를 흡수하는 것을 좋아하고, 키우기 쉽다.

VOCA
spider plants 자주달개비
absorb 흡수하다
carbon dioxide 이산화탄소

015 Suppose that you come home from school to find a cushion torn apart on the living room floor.

해석 학교에서 집에 돌아와 보니 거실 바닥에 쿠션이 찢겨 있는 상황을 가정해 보자.
KILLER
• suppose that S + V ~ : ~라고 가정해 보자
• to find a cushion ~ : 결과를 나타내는 부사적 용법

VOCA
tear apart 찢다, 해체하다

016 Hiding behind a barrier is a normal response we learn at an early age to protect ourselves.

해석 장애물 뒤에 숨는 것은 우리가 어릴 때 배우는 자신을 보호하기 위한 정상적인 반응이다.
KILLER
• 동명사 주어 단수 취급 : is
• a normal response (that) we learn : 목적격 관계대명사의 생략

VOCA
barrier 장벽, 장애물(= obstacle)
response 반응

017 Manufacturers will use the information generated by these smart products to sell you other services.

해석 제조업체들은 당신에게 다른 서비스를 판매하기 위해 이 스마트 제품들에 의해 생성된 정보를 이용할 것이다.
KILLER
• 과거분사 generated ~ products가 the information 수식
• other + 복수명사 services

VOCA
manufacturer 제조업체
generate 발생시키다, 만들어내다

018 A map must distort reality in order to portray a complex, three-dimensional world on a flat sheet of paper.

해석 지도는 복잡한 3차원 세계를 평면 종이에 표현하기 위해 현실을 왜곡해야 한다.
KILLER
in order to V : ~하기 위해(= so as to V)

VOCA
distort 왜곡하다
portray 묘사하다, 표현하다
three-dimensional 3차원의
dimension 크기, 규모, 차원

019 You may say yes to family members who give you a hard time, only to feel frustrated by the lack of time for yourself.

020 19th century astronomers working with the first astronomical cameras were astonished to discover that outer space was much more crowded than they had thought.

내 인생 **마지막 기본 영어구문**

019 You may say yes to family members who give you a hard time, only to feel frustrated by the lack of time for yourself.

:해석: 당신을 힘들게 하는 가족에게 마지못해 yes 라고 말하지만, 결국 자신을 위한 시간이 부족해 답답함을 느끼게 될 것이다.
KILLER
- only to V : 그러나 결국 ~하게 되다
- 감정분사 frustrated

:VOCA:
give a hard time 힘들게 하다
lack 부족

020 19th century astronomers working with the first astronomical cameras were astonished to discover that outer space was much more crowded than they had thought.

:해석: 최초의 천체 카메라를 사용하던 19세기 천문학자들은 우주가 그들이 생각했던 것보다 훨씬 더 붐빈다는 것을 발견하고 깜짝 놀랐다.
KILLER
- working ~ cameras는 astronomers를 후치수식하는 현재분사
- 감정분사 astonished(놀란) = amazed, astounded, startled, shocked
- 암기분사 crowded(붐비는)
- 비교급 강조부사 much

:VOCA:
astronomer 천문학자
astronomical 천체의
astonished 깜짝 놀란
outer space 우주
crowded 붐비는

3 동명사의 여러 가지 형태

① 동명사가 본동사보다 먼저 일어난 일일 경우 having p.p를 사용한다.
② 동명사가 수동의 의미를 나타낼 때는 being p.p를 사용한다.

021 We have the right to state our opinions without the fear of being punished.

022 There are many products which benefit from being touched in some way before being purchased.

023 A currently popular attitude is to blame technology for having brought on the environmental problems.

024 I am concerned about having made mistakes, and the objections of the spectators are still ringing in my ears.

내 인생 마지막 기본 영어구문

021 We have the right to state our opinions without the fear of being punished.

해석 우리는 처벌받을 걱정 없이 우리의 의견을 말할 권리가 있다.
KILLER
수동의 동명사 being punished

VOCA
state 말하다, 언급하다

022 There are many products which benefit from being touched in some way before being purchased.

해석 구매 전에 어떤 식으로든 만져보는 것이 도움이 되는 제품들이 많이 있다.
KILLER
- 수동의 동명사 being touched, being purchased
- in some way 어떤 식으로든

VOCA
beneftit from ~로부터 이익을 얻다

023 A currently popular attitude is to blame technology for having brought on the environmental problems.

해석 현재 대중적인 태도는 환경 문제를 초래한 것에 대해 기술을 탓하는 것이다.
KILLER
- blame A for B : B에 대해 A를 탓하다
- 완료 동명사 having brought on

VOCA
currently 현재의
popular 인기있는, 대중적인, 일반적인
bring on 초래하다

024 I am concerned about having made mistakes, and the objections of the spectators are still ringing in my ears.

해석 나는 실수를 저질렀던 것이 걱정되고, 관중들의 항의가 아직도 귓가에 맴돈다.
KILLER
- be concerned about : ~에 대해 걱정하다
- be concerned with : ~와 관련/관심이 있다
- 완료 동명사 having made

VOCA
objection 항의, 반대
spectator 관중
ring in one's ears 귓가에 울리다

4 분사구문

025 Invited to a dinner party, we feel under pressure to invite our hosts to one of ours.

026 Native to a tropical climate, this leafy tree can survive almost anywhere in the world.

027 The course starts with an indoor lesson, followed by a walk through fields.

028 I forced myself to keep running, my heart beating wildly.

029 The increased flexibility will lengthen your running stride, allowing you to run faster.

030 They had each pulled at the crown, their united strength causing injuries.

025 Invited to a dinner party, we feel under pressure to invite our hosts to one of ours.

해석 파티에 초대를 받으면, 우리도 우리의 것들(파티) 중 하나에 초대한 사람을 초대해야 한다는 부담을 느낀다.
KILLER
- 수동의 분사구문 Invited ~ party
- 소유대명사 ours = our parties

VOCA
feel under pressure 압박을 느끼다
host 주최자, 초대한 사람

026 Native to a tropical climate, this leafy tree can survive almost anywhere in the world.

해석 열대 기후가 원산인 이 무성한 나무는 세계 거의 어디서나 생존할 수 있다.
KILLER
- 분사구문 (Being) Native ~ climate
- 타동사 survive + 목적어

VOCA
native to ~가 원산인
tropical 열대인
leafy (잎이) 무성한

027 The course starts with an indoor lesson, followed by a walk through fields.

해석 이 과정은 실내 수업으로 시작되며, 그 뒤에는 들판 걷기가 이어진다.
KILLER
수동의 분사구문 followed ~ fields

VOCA
course 과정
indoor 실내의

028 I forced myself to keep running, my heart beating wildly.

해석 나는 계속 달리도록 자신을 다그쳤고, 내 심장은 거칠게 뛰고 있었다.
KILLER
- 5형식 force A to V (A가 V하도록 강요하다)
- 3형식 keep Ving (계속해서 ~하다)
- 독립분사구문 my heart ~ wildly

VOCA
beat wildly 거칠게 뛰다

029 The increased flexibility will lengthen your running stride, allowing you to run faster.

해석 증가한 유연성은 너의 보폭을 길게 만들고, 그래서 네가 더 빠르게 달릴 수 있게 만든다.
KILLER
능동의 분사구문 allowing ~ faster

VOCA
increased 증가한
flexibility 유연성
lengthen 길게 만들다, 늘이다
stride 보폭

030 They had each pulled at the crown, their united strength causing injuries.

해석 그들은 모두 왕관을 잡아당겼고, 그들의 합쳐진 힘이 부상을 초래했다.
KILLER
독립분사구문 their ~ injuries

VOCA
pull at ~를 잡아당기다
crown 왕관
united 결집된, 합쳐진
strength 힘
injury 부상

031 The other brother, filled with regret, chose to stay in the village and try to make amends for his offenses.

032 When threatened, short-horned lizards are capable of blowing up their bodies up to twice their normal size.

033 Having studied your case, it seems that your cancellation request was sent to us after the authorized cancellation period.

034 Throughout history, unpaid amateurs, working for their communities, have made remarkable achievements in a wide variety of fields.

035 Workers are trained to do their jobs in an efficient way to meet organizational goals while ignoring other important matters related to their health.

031 The other brother, filled with regret, chose to stay in the village and try to make amends for his offenses.

> 해석 : 후회를 가득 안은 다른 형제는 마을에 남아 자신의 잘못을 바로잡기로 했다.

KILLER
- 수동의 분사구문 filled with regret
- 3형식 choose to V (~하는 것을 선택하다)
- 3형식 try to V (~하기 위해 노력하다)

VOCA
make amends for ~을 보상하다
(= make up for, compensate for)
amend 개정하다, 수정하다
Amendment 미국 헌법 수정 조항, 수정안
offense 잘못, 죄

032 When threatened, short-horned lizards are capable of blowing up their bodies up to twice their normal size.

> 해석 : 위협을 받으면, 짧은 뿔 도마뱀은 몸을 원래 크기의 두 배까지 부풀릴 수 있다.

KILLER
- 수동의 분사구문 when threatened
- be capable of Ving = be able to V
- twice the 명사 : ~의 두 배

VOCA
lizard 도마뱀
blow up 부풀리다

033 Having studied your case, it seems that your cancellation request was sent to us after the authorized cancellation period.

> 해석 : 당신의 사례를 검토해 보니, 취소 요청이 허가된 기간 이후에 접수된 것으로 보입니다.

KILLER
- 완료 분사구문 Having ~ case
- it seems that S + V : ~인 것처럼 보이다

VOCA
cancellation request 취소 요청
authorized 허가된
period 기간

034 Throughout history, unpaid amateurs, working for their communities, have made remarkable achievements in a wide variety of fields.

> 해석 : 역사를 통틀어, 지역사회를 위해 일하는 무급 아마추어들이 다양한 분야에서 놀라운 업적을 이루어 왔다.

KILLER
능동의 분사구문 working ~ communities

VOCA
throughout ~전반에 걸쳐, ~내내
unpaid 무급의
community 공동체
remarkable 놀라운
a variety of 다양한

035 Workers are trained to do their jobs in an efficient way to meet organizational goals while ignoring other important matters related to their health.

> 해석 : 근로자들은 건강과 관련된 중요한 문제들을 무시한 채 조직의 목표를 달성하기 위해 효율적으로 일하도록 훈련받는다.

KILLER
- be trained to V : ~하도록 훈련받다
- 능동의 분사구문 while ignoring ~ health
- matters를 후치수식하는 과거분사 related ~ health
- another 단수명사 vs. other 복수명사

VOCA
efficient 효율적인
organizational 조직의
meet goals 목표를 달성하다
related to ~와 관련된

036 The package consisted of a paper bag with cord running through it.

037 One is leaning back in his chair with his eyes closed and his feet on the desk.

038 With Hoy being such a loved player, the crowds would wave their arms to cheer for him.

039 The American Coots migrate from August to December, with males moving south before the females and their babies.

036 The package consisted of a paper bag with cord running through it.

해석 그 꾸러미는 끈이 꿰어져 있는 종이봉투로 구성되어 있었다.

KILLER
with 부대상황 분사구문

VOCA
package 소포, 꾸러미, 포장
consist of ~로 구성되다
cord 끈
run through 관통하다

037 One is leaning back in his chair with his eyes closed and his feet on the desk.

해석 누군가가 눈을 감고 발을 책상에 둔 채로 의자에 기대어 앉아 있었다.

KILLER
with 부대상황 분사구문

VOCA
lean back 뒤로 기대다

038 With Hoy being such a loved player, the crowds would wave their arms to cheer for him.

해석 Hoy는 매우 사랑받는 선수였기 때문에, 관중들은 그를 응원하기 위해 팔을 흔들곤 했다.

KILLER
- with 부대상황 분사구문
- so 형 a 명 vs. such a 형 명 : 매우 (형용사)한 (명사)
- would = used to RV : ~하곤 했다

VOCA
crowd 대중, 사람들
loved 사랑받는
cheer for 응원하다

039 The American Coots migrate from August to December, with males moving south before the females and their babies.

해석 아메리카물닭은 수컷들이 암컷과 새끼들의 앞에서 남쪽으로 움직이는 상태로 8월부터 12월까지 이동한다.

KILLER
with 부대상황 분사구문

VOCA
migrate 이동하다, 이주하다

EXERCISE

(본동사 VS. 분사)

다음 문장의 옳고 그름을 판단하고, 옳지 않은 부분은 옳게 고치시오. (01~07)

01 The explosion of personal liberty creating a lot of options that our ancestors never faced.

02 After his death, a law restricted the number of terms a president could serve was passed.

03 The most common activity among people observed by Owen turning out to be watching other people.

04 When a human being walks, his or her arms and legs moving in a specific way in relation to his or her body.

ANSWER

01 The explosion of personal liberty creating a lot of options that our ancestors never faced.

정답 creating → created
해설 주어인 the explosion에 이어지는 주절 동사가 없다.
해석 개인의 자유가 폭발적으로 증가하면서, 우리 조상들이 겪어보지 못한 많은 선택지를 만들어냈다.
KILLER
목적격 관계대명사 that + face의 목적어가 빠진 불완전한 문장

VOCA
explosion 폭발, 증가
liberty 자유
option 선택지
ancestor 조상
face 직면하다

02 After his death, a law restricted the number of terms a president could serve was passed.

정답 restricted → restricting
해설 주절의 동사는 was passed이다. restricted ~ serve는 a law를 후치수식하는 분사여야 하고, 타동사 restrict가 목적어와 함께 쓰였으므로 능동의 현재분사인 restricting이 적절하다.
해석 그가 죽은 후, 대통령이 재임할 수 있는 횟수를 제한하는 법이 통과되었다.
KILLER
• restricting ~ serve는 a law를 후치수식하는 능동의 현재분사
• terms (that) a president could serve : 목적격 관계대명사의 생략

VOCA
restrict 제한하다
term (1) 기간, 임기, 학기
　　　(2) 용어, 단어
serve (공직을) 맡다

03 The most common activity among people observed by Owen turning out to be watching other people.

정답 turning → turned
해설 주절에 동사가 없다. 주어인 the most common activity에 연결할 수 있도록 turn out을 본동사 형태로 수정한다.
해석 Owen이 관찰한 사람들 사이에서 가장 흔한 활동은 다른 사람들을 지켜보는 것이었다.
KILLER
• observed by Owen은 the most common activity를 후치수식하는 과거분사
• turn out (to be) 명/형: ~인 것으로 드러나다

VOCA
observe 관찰하다

04 When a human being walks, his or her arms and legs moving in a specific way in relation to his or her body.

정답 moving → move
해설 주절에 동사가 없다. 주어인 his or her arms and legs에 연결할 수 있도록 moving을 본동사 형태로 수정한다.
해석 사람이 걸을 때, 팔과 다리는 몸과 관련하여 특정한 방식으로 움직인다.

VOCA
in relation to ~에 관하여, 관련하여

05 Organs can begin to fail and the chemical reactions that power the body become less efficient.

06 The volcanic ash, after blasting high into the atmosphere, presenting a risk to the engines of airplanes.

07 People who regularly exercise three times a week for thirty minutes living longer than people who are inactive.

ANSWER

05 Organs can begin to fail and the chemical reactions that power the body become less efficient.

정답 O

해설 장기들은 기능을 멈추기 시작할 수 있고 몸에 에너지를 공급하는 화학 반응들은 덜 효율적으로 변한다.

KILLER
- 목적격 관계대명사 that power the body는 reactions를 후치수식한다.
- 2형식 become + 형용사 efficient

VOCA
organ 장기
chemical reaction 화학 반응
efficient 효율적인

06 The volcanic ash, after blasting high into the atmosphere, presenting a risk to the engines of airplanes.

정답 presenting → presented

해설 주절에 동사가 없다. 주어인 The volcanic ash에 연결할 수 있도록 presenting을 본동사 형태로 수정한다.

해석 화산재는 대기권 위로 치솟은 후 비행기 엔진에 위험을 초래한다.

VOCA
ash 재
blast 폭발하다, 치솟다
atmosphere 대기, 공중
present 초래하다, 제시하다, 제출하다

07 People who regularly exercise three times a week for thirty minutes living longer than people who are inactive.

정답 living → live

해설 주절에 동사가 없다. 주어인 People에 연결할 수 있도록 living을 본동사 형태로 수정한다.

해석 일주일에 세 번씩 30분 동안 규칙적으로 운동하는 사람들은 활동하지 않는 사람들보다 오래 산다.

KILLER
- 주격 관계대명사 who ~ minutes는 people을 후치수식한다.
- 비교급 longer + than

VOCA
regularly 주기적으로
inactive 비활동적인, 움직이지 않는

김태은

주요 약력

현) 노량진 박문각 공무원 영어 온라인, 오프라인 교수
전) 노량진 에듀윌 공무원 학원
    노량진 아모르이그잼 공무원 학원
    신림 황남기 스파르타 학원
    지텔프 코리아

주요 저서

박문각 공무원 김태은 영어 마지막 기본 영문법
박문각 공무원 김태은 영어 마지막 기본 영어구문

김태은 영어
마지막 기본 영어구문

초판 인쇄 | 2025. 9. 10.   **초판 발행** | 2025. 9. 15.   **편저** | 김태은
발행인 | 박 용   **발행처** | (주)박문각출판   **등록** | 2015년 4월 29일 제2019-000137호
주소 | 06654 서울시 서초구 효령로 283 서경 B/D 4층   **팩스** | (02)584-2927
전화 | 교재 문의 (02)6466-7202

저자와의 협의하에 인지생략

이 책의 무단 전재 또는 복제 행위를 금합니다.

정가 15,000원
ISBN 979-11-7519-113-6